YOHO

A HISTORY AND CELEBRATION
OF YOHO NATIONAL PARK

YOHO

A HISTORY AND CELEBRATION OF YOHO NATIONAL PARK

by R.W.Sandford

This book is a project
of the
Friends of Yoho National Park

Front Cover:
Mt. Burgess provides the backdrop
in this view of Emerald Lake.

© 1993 Altitude Publishing Canada Ltd.

1408 Railway Ave.,
P.O. Box 1410,
Canmore, Alberta T0L 0M0.

**Canadian Cataloguing
in Publication Data**
Sandford, Robert W.
Yoho

ISBN 1-55153-002-3

1. Yoho National Park (B.C.)--History.
2. Natural history--British Columbia--
Yoho National Park.
I. Title.
FC3814.Y65S35 1993
971.1'68
C93-091697-2
F1089.Y65S35 1993

The publisher is grateful to the Friends of
Yoho National Park for all their help in
the production of this book.

Editor: Nancy Flight
Design: Steve Penner

Made in Western Canada
Printed and bound in Western Canada
by Friesen Printers, Altona, Manitoba,
using Canadian-made paper and
vegetable-based inks.

Altitude GreenTree Program
Altitude will plant in Western Canada
twice as many trees as were used in the
manufacturing of this book.

The Publisher gratefully
acknowledges the assistance of the
Alberta Foundation for the Arts,
and the Department of
Communications Book Industry
Development Program.

Friends of Yoho
Box 100
Field, B.C. V0A 1G0

The Friends of Yoho Society is a non-profit association
that cooperates with Yoho National Park to promote
understanding and enjoyment of the park. The association
is interested in preserving the human and railway history of
the area promoting an awareness of the natural environment in
Yoho National Park, and making a visit to the park more enjoyable.
As a cooperating association we operate a retail outlet in Yoho Park
selling items which reflect the natural and human history of Yoho, as well as
publish guide books, maps, and historical material concerning the park. The restoration of
an historic railway building to be used as a museum is a long term goal of the association.

CONTENTS

....

....

In English, the native word "yoho" means "wonder".
This is a book about wonder.
From mountain to stream, from fossil to Field,
from back-country to the main highway,
Yoho National Park is a wondrous place.
Although Yoho is a wild and rugged mountain landscape,
its history is rich with human drama and struggle.
It is a story about adventurers, climbers and explorers.
It is a book about builders and railway men, surveyors and scientists.
And it is a book about the people who truly love and care for
one of the world's most wondrous of places.

ACKNOWLEDGMENTS

....

For Gordon and Bev Rutherford, through whose friendship
we learned the wonder of Yoho.

This book originates in my personal experience of Yoho National Park. Personal experience, however, is seldom enough of a motivation for writing a book. Many thousands experience Yoho each year but few write about how this remarkable place affected them. I am indebted to many people for their direct and indirect encouragement in the writing of this appreciation of the park. This book would not have been conceived without the enthusiasm of The Friends of Yoho and their commitment to the history and living culture of Yoho National Park. This book would not have been written without the encouragement of Vi Sandford and her constant support in the researching, writing, and editing that were necessary to translate a personal sense of place into a final, publishable form. Much also is owed to Nancy Flight, who edited the manuscript on behalf of the publisher.

This work, however, was not simply a literary endeavour. Acknowledgment must extend beyond inspiration and production to include a number of remarkable people who, over many years, have refused to allow the detailed history of Yoho to disappear through neglect. Foremost among these was Pat Rutherford, who, for much of her adult life, kept up a lively correspondence with old-timers and others who had left Field for gentler winters in most hospitable climes. Fortunately for this history, Pat was not above pulling historic documents relating to the park out of waste paper baskets. Nor was she reluctant in any way to share all she knew and had with me. Although it hardly does credit to all she has done for the history of Yoho, it is my hope that this book at least pays tribute to the enduring spirit of place and community she left in her wake in Yoho. Similar acknowledgment must go to Glen and Irene Brook, who gave life to the more recent history of Yoho by way of their loving re-creation of many of the people who shaped it. Much is owed, too, to Mary Decicco Roberts and the others who allowed the author to explore their family histories in Yoho. Thanks are due also to the Whyte Museum of the Canadian Rockies and C. P. Archives, who have granted the use of photographs in this book. Finally, thanks must go to the Canadian Parks Service, whose support for this project was complete and unflagging.

INVOCATION

....

The town of Field nestles beneath Mt. Stephen.
The Kicking Horse River runs through the foreground.

Yoho: An Inquiry after Wonder

Field is the capital city of Yoho National Park. We arrived there in May. Most of the snow had disappeared in town but still lingered in deep drifts in the trees that rose like green surf up the nearly vertical walls of the surrounding valley. The dark, just-thawed earth smelled of mud, grass, and pine needles. The potholes on the dirt streets were filled with still, brown water that reflected the bruised blue of the sky. It was silent save for the rising and falling thrum of traffic coming from the highway across the river.

We had been warned about Field. Field distinguishes itself from other mountain towns by the fact that it is difficult to live in, so you have to want to be there to make it work for you. In the other national park towns in the Rockies there is plenty to do if you do not like to hike or ski or climb. In Banff, for example, you could live in the company of thousands of other people who

7

do not particularly care about mountains. Unlike Fielders, many Banff residents could live anywhere. Life in Field is clearly and almost exclusively focused on the surrounding park. You have to have more than a passing interest in the landscape to make living there tolerable.

For its part, the landscape is stunning. If anything, one could argue that there is too much landscape and that in Field you are too close to it. Living in

Storms called "Yoho Blows" punctuate the already lengthy Rocky Mountain winter. The long Yoho winters add to the preciousness of each day of the mountain summer.

Field is like living in the bottom of a canyon. Not just any canyon, but the Grand Canyon. It is 2 kilometres — more than a vertical mile — from the river that slides along the bottom of the valley floor to the summits of the peaks that loom over the town. The mountains are so close and so huge that all you can see out of most of the windows in town are the trees at their bases. We moved into a smaller old saltbox next to the train tracks. You had to walk all the way out of the house and crane your neck as far you could to see the dizzying summit of Mt. Stephen right next to the house. Without the aid of binoculars, you could sit on the porch and watch mountain goats as they carefully picked their way along ledges on the steep cliffs of Mt. Burgess.

Like it or not elk were in the yard all year round. People stayed alert when they took out the garbage or went to the post office to get their mail. It was not uncommon to find a black bear or a grizzly on the street. Or a bull elk in rut. Or a coyote after a stray dog.

In summer it rained. In winter it snowed and snowed and snowed. Often there were local blizzards called Yoho blows that could bury a one-story house in drifted snow. The country could get to you, and if it didn't, the highway would. Driving in and out of the valley you faced two serious hazards. Ice, snow, avalanche, and mud and rock slides on the steep and winding hills were one hazard — the country leaning in on you again. The other hazard was other drivers. Inexperienced urbanites in motor homes wandered all over the road in summer, and in winter, downhill skiers turned the road into the equivalent of a North Pole Grand Prix. Every time you pulled up to the edge of the highway you thought of these hazards. Most Fielders had either seen a fatal highway crash or had had a life-threatening incident on the Trans-Canada Highway. The highway and all its terrors were part of life in the mountains and part of living in Field. So it was that people came and went from this town, staying as long as it took to solidify a job with the government or the railway, and leaving when the weather, the isolation, or the highway became completely unbearable.

People who live in Field for a long time come to grips with the hazards of the highway. They wait out the bad weather and persist through sometimes-stormy relations with other locals that are often a part of life in this tightly knit town. In time, they acquire a certain grace that comes from having accepted the often-difficult terms demanded by a land turned completely on end. When you gradually stop fighting the roads and the weather, a different Yoho begins to preside in your mind.

When we first moved to Field, I felt for a time that I was the only one in town who did not have all the life skills needed to live successfully there. I was taught a great deal by my neighbors, who, it appears, viewed me on as something of a rehabilitation project. Under their guidance, I learned to clean a chimney, shovel a roof, and even fall a tree if need be. Although at no point was I beyond throwing a log through the back window of my pickup truck, I gradually became accomplished enough to cut my own firewood. Although none of my neighbors ever liked to watch me split this wood, I was slowly accepted, blemishes and all, into the community of Field. Over this time, I gradually realized that many of the attitudes and much of the behavior of the locals had in some subtle way been shaped by the mountains around them. This, I discovered, even began to happen to me.

Given time, the landscape around us shapes us. Native North Americans knew that. All the old-time park wardens understood it. So did the early horse packers and guides. In Field we were all subjects of the weather and the season. Even our moods were shaped by the kinds of clouds that obscured the thin strip of blue, that narrow slit of sky above the town. Houses in Field were small

9

so that they would be easier to heat. Almost all of them had wood heaters to augment propane furnaces. Since fuel was very expensive, people put on more clothes when it got cold rather than just turning up the heat. Fashionable but impractical clothes were seldom worn by Fielders. All the people in town wore roughly the same kinds of wool shirts, winter jackets and boots, warm hats and gloves, sometimes even in summer. We all looked pretty much the same. It was rather like an ethnic costume fashioned by the gradual acceptance of local mountain weather. The same sensible attitude existed toward automobiles. Very few people in Field bought expensive, luxurious cars. A practical vehicle bought at a reasonable price was a sign of good sense. I remember being teased for buying a two-year-old station wagon because it was too new. Ownership of an expensive urban status symbol could hurt your reputation in town.

The object of all these compromises was to allow you to create a self-reinforcing lifestyle. Living in Field could be relatively cheap if you adopted a simple way of life. The less it cost you to live, the more time you had at your disposal. The more time you had at your disposal, the more places you could travel, inside and outside the park. The more places you travelled, the more the country could grow in you. The more the country grew in you, the fewer your material needs and the more simply you could live. It was a way of living that fed on itself. Many people in Field had completely mastered this mountain way of life. They lived simply, but very elegantly. They read widely in winter, and walked or biked or climbed just as widely in summer. They had time for the country, and the country had time for them. Unlike harried visitors who raised their clenched fists to the wet skies, locals seldom worried about the weather. There were almost always enough clear and perfect days to travel in, and if there weren't, you just dressed for the rain. It was with this enlightenment that my inquiry after wonder really began.

Although it was easy to see who had mastered a simple way of life, it was more difficult to measure how much any given local had been affected by the wonder that is the basis of the park's name and spirit. It is my experience that a deep, carefully developed appreciation of place is not something worn as a badge on the outside of somebody's coat. It is not a degree you can get, or a trophy you can show your friends. It is not something you could directly ask about. In the people I met in Field who most certainly had a keenly developed relationship with the park, sense of place displayed itself more as an attitude than anything else. For example, an old-time park warden named Glen Brook had a unique sense of Yoho 40 years before I met him. The wonder he possessed manifested itself in a keen naturalist's eye, an almost-photographic knowledge of the park's backcountry, and a gentleness and unselfish charm that easily made him the town's most famous local. His wife, Irene, had the same charm. Their friend Slim Haugen had it too, a timeless, fluid grace instilled by the land. Gordon Rutherford, born and raised in Field, had this same gentleness and profound sense of place. He too possessed an astounding memory of important things that happened, it seemed, on every peak and in every valley. In explaining the history of the park, Gordon was simply retelling the events of his life as it unfolded among these peaks. This was true too for his wife, Bev. Randall Robertson, who had spent most of his working life in Yoho, had the same easy grace. So did Sid Brook and his brother Alec. So did Brian Hall. So did Men Camastral. So did Pierre Lemire and 40 others who lived in that small town. All of these people smiled easily and gave hospitality freely. They tended to care a lot for those who loved their land. A sense of community meant a lot to them too. So, here we have it. A sense of place is a form of grace. It is a way of refining yourself by giving yourself up to the country you live in.

A sense of place is acquired in increments. It takes years to shape. To truly see wonder in any place, one has to experience it through the seasons, through years of subtle learning that comes only from cumulative observation. One has to bathe in the country, in its spring creeks, in its summer lakes, in its autumn larches, and in the howling winds of its bitter winters. The legend and legacy of the land are derived only partly from the rock walls and waterfalls. The ways of properly and fully experiencing the country are passed on, generation to generation, by those who have lived on and loved the land. If there is wonder in Yoho, it is because people put it there. These mountains are special because those who have lived among them have made them so and would not have them any other way.

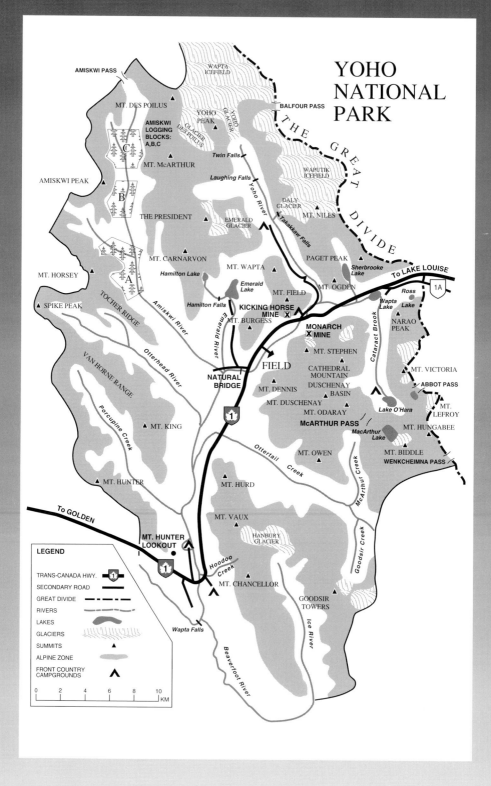

Chapter 1
....

The Geography of Wonder

A century ago, along the Great Divide in British Columbia, a national park was created and named after a native exclamation for indescribable wonderment. Applied by natives first to the river and then to the valley through which the river runs, yoho is a word describing reverence tinged with fear inspired by the sublime. For the Cree, "Yoho!" was an expression of the profoundest awe. Suggesting the sacred and the mysterious, yoho was applied by the Cree to those rare and powerful natural places that could induce a mind-slowing sense of aesthetic arrest. In its simplest translation, yoho means wonder.

Even a century ago, when much of the West was still wild, Yoho stood out. On this continent, perhaps only Yosemite has as many spectacular natural features in such a small area. The scale and presence of Yoho's peaks and valleys gave visitors an immediate and unforgettable sense of place. Its rock walls and waterfalls captured the soul. Yoho became one of Canada's earliest national parks, and those who experienced it often yearned to return. Although it is perhaps a curious word, yoho aptly describes the wonder that can be experienced there.

The Map Of Yoho

Most visitors first see Yoho in the shape of a map. Maps are important. A single glance at a good map can tell you a great deal. We learn the topography of place - how it has been shaped by restless forces within and without the planet. Topographic lines tell us how irregular the land's surface is. In the case of Yoho, the lines tell us how steep the walls of the mountains are, and to what altitude they poke into the sky. A topographical map will tell us where the rivers flow, what grades they flow down, and the size of the area they drain. Though it may not tell us what animals live in this land, the map does tell us where we might, at least, begin to look for them. A good map will illustrate where the trees are, the altitudes at which they grow, and what exists above them. The topographical map of Yoho tells us where glaciers and icefields are, so we may plot our own routes to view them. But a topographical map is more

Takakkaw Falls is the second highest waterfall in Canada and one of the most popular features in Yoho National Park. It is located in the Yoho Valley.

than just geography. The map also places us amidst names. Some of the places names in Yoho are magically descriptive. Ice River, Waterfall Valley, and Laughing Falls tell us what scenery to expect and even how we might feel if we visited them. We rightly suspect that mountains with names like Van Horne and Deville may be named for people. In divulging this, the map tells us that people made a place for themselves here; that people are part of the history of Yoho. We wonder who these people were. Who was Burgess? Who was Owen? Who was Dennis? Who was King? The map becomes a mystery we want to solve.

On the official maps of the four Rocky Mountain national parks, Yoho is a small, irregular diamond tucked between Banff National Park on the east and Kootenay National Park on the south. Glaciers and icefields form its northeast boundary which it shares with Banff. Here, amid the Waputik Mountains, lie the Waputik and Wapta icefields. Waputik is a Stoney word meaning "mountain goat." It is out of this icefield that the Daly Glacier flows. The Daly Glacier and nearby Mount Daly were named in 1916 by the American climber Charles

Fay for his friend Joseph Francis Daly, who had served as president of the American Geographical Society in New York. Melt from the Daly Glacier forms Takakkaw Falls, one of Yoho's most spectacular natural features. Takakkaw is another native expression of wonderment. In the Stoney language it means "it is magnificent." Wapta is also a Stoney word, meaning "running water," and lots of that pours from the many glaciers that flow from this large icefield. The Waputik and Wapta icefields straddle the Great Divide between Yoho and Banff national parks. The Great Divide separates waters that flow to the Arctic Ocean in the east, and the Pacific Ocean in the west.

Studying the map more fully, one also observes the presence of four dense blocks of topographical lines that indicate that at least half the park is at or above timberline. In the north, the President Range, composed of 12 named peaks, separates the Amiskwi Valley from the valley of the Yoho River. Four of the peaks in the President Range, the President, the Vice President, Mt. Marpole, and Mt. Kerr, are named for early Canadian Pacific Railway officials who worked in the mountain West.

South and west of the President Range, but still north of the Trans-Canada Highway, is a smaller massif composed of Mts. King and Deville. Mt. King was named by provincial land surveyor Otto Klotz for William Frederick King, who was, among other things, a member of Canada's famous international boundary survey between 1908 and 1916. Mt. Deville was named for another famous surveyor, Édouard-Gaston Deville. While surveyor general of Canada, Deville rocketed Canada's infant Dominion Land Surveys to the forefront of surveying science through the pioneering use of photogrammetry in map making. Photogrammetry is the technical name for the science of making reliable measurements of distance through the use of photographs. Mt. King and Mt. Deville form part of the Van Horne Range, which extends out of the park into the province. Mt. Hunter is also part of this group. Mt. Hunter was named by an early explorer, James Hector, for either Archdeacon James Hunter, who was an Anglican missionary among the Cree, or John Hunter, a Scottish anatomist and surgeon.

South of the Van Horne Range is a horseshoe-shaped mass of very high mountains in the southwestern part of the park surrounding the Ice River. This very beautiful group of peaks includes a glacier and 15 named mountains. Among them are the twin towers of Mt. Goodsir, the highest peaks wholly within the park. The Goodsir Towers were named by James Hector for two brothers he knew who were doctors in Edinburgh, Scotland.

Finally, a great circle of peaks clusters around Cataract Creek and Lake O'Hara on the eastern boundary of Yoho. Here the land stands on end. This wonderful area is regarded as one of the most interesting and engaging places in all of the Rocky Mountains.

Yoho contains 10 river valleys that provide relief to the peaks that surround them and water to the Kicking Horse River. It is in these valleys that the mountain forests grow. The valley of the Kicking Horse River, through which the Trans-Canada Highway and the main line of the Canadian Pacific Railway have been constructed, and the Amiskwi Valley are the largest valleys in the park. The Yoho and Emerald rivers also join the Kicking Horse from the north and, when swollen with melt, are powerful rivers too. The other forested valleys north of the Kicking Horse River include the valley drained by Porcupine Creek just west of the Van Horne Range and the Otterhead River Valley, a narrow, wild defile seldom visited even by people who work for the park. South of the Kicking Horse at the west end of the park are the Beaverfoot River, which flows into the Kicking Horse just below Wapta Falls, and the Ice River, which together form much of the park's southern boundary. These two valleys are also heavily forested. Two other major drainage basins exist in Yoho: the Ottertail River, which bisects the southern half of the park, and Cataract Creek, which drains the Lake O'Hara area.

Thus, Yoho National Park is roughly divided into three geographical provinces. Forested valley floors at the lowest altitudes comprise a little less than half of the park's 1313 square kilometres, 507 square miles. Large regions of upended mountains, composed mostly of bare, frost-shattered rock, comprise about half of Yoho. Finally, high plateaus composed of accumulating icefield snows and living glaciers make up the remaining 10 percent of the wonder.

The presence of glacier ice, the altitude of the peaks, and the number of watercourses draining the area imply regular precipitation in summer and heavy snow in winter. The large percentage of the landscape that exists above the altitudinal line at which trees cease to grow implies that at high elevations, at least, the climate often resembles that of the poles of the Earth. As the earliest explorers quickly discovered, Yoho is often cold, wet, windy, and just plain miserable to travel in. The earliest explorers, surveyors, railway engineers, and mountain climbers might add one additional element to this preliminary

The Daly Glacier. This glacier is a small part of a large icefield complex that 1.5 lies along the Great Divide between Yoho and Banff National Parks. Two views are shown, the first taken in 1981 and the second taken in 1992. The recession of this glacier during that decade is highly noticeable. Glaciers can be used as instruments measuring the effects of global warming.

description of Yoho: besides being stunningly beautiful, Yoho could be very dangerous too.

The Palliser Expedition

The first geographer and one of the earliest Europeans to visit the mountains that are now part of Yoho National Park was James Hector. Hector was the surgeon for a British expedition led by John Palliser that visited Canada between 1857 and 1860 to study the geography and geology of the West and to determine its mineral and agricultural potential. Hector was both a skilled medical doctor and a competent surveyor. He had also studied geology under the most progressive earth scientists of his time and was required by the terms and conditions of his assignment to post regular geological reports to none other than Sir Rodney Murchison, one of the most prominent of all of Victorian scientists. Although Hector was interested in the geological evolution of mountainous landscapes, his principal task in the Rockies was to determine if a wagon road could be built from the Red River along the Saskatchewan River through British Columbia to the Pacific coast. Making sense of this jumbled, shattered land was not a simple task. Hector immersed himself in the country for months at a time, learning the lay of the land and mastering the difficulties of travelling through it. His observations and the expedition's maps of the mountain region became a foundation for ideas about the processes of mountain building in the Yoho Rockies.

Captain Palliser and his men were charged by the British Secretary of State to explore "that portion of British North America which lies between the northern branch of the River Saskatchewan and the frontier of the United States, and between the Red River and the Rocky Mountains." They were given complete instructions about what route to take across eastern Canada to Fort Garry. Instructions were less specific about the route the expedition was to take from Red River to the Rockies:

> *At the commencement of the season of 1858 you will start, as soon as the weather is sufficiently open and favourable, to explore the country between the two branches of the Saskatchewan River and south of the southern branch, and thence proceeding westward to the head waters of that river, you will endeavour, from the best information you can collect, to ascertain whether one or more practicable passes exist over the Rocky Mountains within British territory, and south of that known to exist between Mt. Hooker and Brown.*

The pass mentioned between Mts. Hooker and Brown is Athabasca Pass, discovered by David Thompson in January of 1811. At the time of the Palliser Expedition, it was still the main pass used in the national walking and canoeing route across Canada.

After warning the party not to become involved in any wars between Native groups, the expedition's official instructions stated that if the party went all the way to the Pacific coast rather than returning to the Red River before undertaking the homeward trip to England, the cost of the return voyage would come out of the expedition members' own pockets. The Secretary of State's final instructions urged Palliser not to spend too much money:

I have to request that you will communicate to me, for the information of the Lords Commissioners of the Treasury, the mode in which the expenditure incurred by you while in the territories under control of the Hudson's Bay Company is to be defrayed, and that you will understand that the limits of expense prescribed for the Expedition cannot be exceeded unless under circumstances of urgent necessity, which you will at once report for the information of Her Majesty's Government.

Hector Searches for a Pass

It was August of 1858. After a year of travelling across Canada, Hector was well accustomed to long days in the saddle in unfamiliar country and was looking forward to the new discoveries he would make in the shining mountains he had come so far to explore. As planned, the other members of the Palliser party had already set out on separate, independent expeditions, looking for new passes through the Rockies. John Palliser had headed south from Old Bow Fort toward what is now the Kananaskis area, and Thomas Blakiston was following the Livingstone Range south toward what is now Waterton. Hector himself aimed for the Great Divide, which he eventually hoped to follow north, peeking between mountains for evidence of anything resembling a pass, before heading east to Fort Edmonton, where he would stay the winter.

It is unlikely that when Hector set out from Old Bow Fort on that August day long ago he saw himself as an agent in the greater history of human ideas. He might have known, however, that even without venturing into the Rockies, members of the Palliser Expedition had explored enough country to make a solid historical name for itself. But if the Palliser Expedition was successful, it was because it was composed of dedicated and competent people who enjoyed the challenges of exploration and wanted to get every minute's worth of experience out of their journey to Canada. It would not have mattered what government orders they received; they were going to do this expedition up in style.

On August 11, 1858, Hector, expedition botanist Eugène Bourgeau, a Native hunter named "the one with the thumb like a blunt arrow" (whom Hector called Nimrod), a métis guide named Peter Erasmus, and two horse packers from Red River named Sutherland and Brown left Old Bow Fort with eight horses, headed for the gap in the mountains to the west. The Bow alley cut through five parallel ranges of mountains composed of fossil-bearing lime-

James Hector was the surgeon and geologist of the Palliser Expedition which explored and surveyed much of Western Canada between 1857 and 1859. Hector is credited with being the first recorded European to visit the valley of the Kicking Horse River which he named. (Photo courtesy of the Whyte Museum of the Canadian Rockies.)

stones. Bourgeau named two of the prominent surrounding peaks Grotto and Pigeon mountains. They then followed the narrowing valley between Mt. Rundle and a peak the Natives called "place where the water falls." In his official account to the Secretary of State, posted from Fort Edmonton the following October, Hector explained that he left Bourgeau behind at a "windy" mountain, which was later named for Bourgeau, so that the latter could gather botanical specimens. Three days later he had proceeded up the valley past the "Sawback" range to "Castle" Mount, both of which he named. Hector spent part of a day describing the deep vertical strata of Castle Mountain and, after dressing out a moose they had killed, followed native advice about the most promising pass routes across the divide and entered Vermilion Pass. Hector's keen geological eye immediately discerned the different rock types of the peaks that formed the great divide of the Rockies:

T*he mountains now begin to wear a different aspect, more massive, and evidently much loftier. They are composed of white and pink quartzose sandstone, almost passing into quartzite in some parts, and in others into a fine conglomerate.*

It took the party 6 hours to reach the summit of the divide. After naming Mt. Ball and Mt. Lefroy, two giants that stood out distantly on either side of the pass, Hector began to descend the pass into the Vermilion River Valley. After several days of exploration, Hector surmised that a road could indeed be built down this pass. Hector also noted that there was considerable confusion in Native accounts about the names of the two watercourses in this area. Hector chose to use the name Vermilion River for the watercourse he had followed down Vermilion Pass. The name Kootenay River he applied to the river into which the Vermilion flowed after passing through what is now called Hector Gorge. As much as Hector would have liked to investigate the lower reaches of the Kootenay, he was mindful of the Secretary of State's instructions to return to

The Goodsirs are the highest mountains in Yoho National Park. James Hector described them during his visit to the park in the summer of 1858.

Fort Edmonton by early October. Instead, he ascended the Kootenay River to its headwaters and passed over another divide into the drainage of the Beaverfoot River, which he reached on August 27. This area is now part of the province of British Columbia, lying along the common border between Kootenay and Yoho national parks. Hector's description of the journey from this point, which is the only available account of what happened to him during that first visit to the land of wonder, is contained in the official Papers Relative to the Exploration by Captain Palliser presented to both houses of the British Parliament in June 1859:

> *Ascending the Kootanie River, therefore, on the 27th, I reached a height of land which divides it from one of the principal tributaries of the Columbia River, called Beaver Foot River. The watershed is in a large morass, with several lakes occupying the bottom of a deep wide valley, common to the two streams, although flowing in opposite directions. The line of watershed is so little marked that it is impossible to cross even on foot between the two streams without going into water. On either side of it the stream is dilated into wide shallow lakes, the surfaces of which were crowded with the gaudy flower of Nuphar lutea [yellow water lilies]….*
>
> *…. On the north side of the valley are Mount Goodsir and Pyramid Mountain, and on the south is the Brisco range, which although of no great*

elevation (about 2000 feet above the eye) run, as an unbroken wall, to S.S.E. My Indian declared that the river we had now struck was the head of the north branch of the Saskatchewan, and wished to follow it down, but if my barometer and sympiesometer [an early surveying device] were acting with any accuracy we were now about on a level with what I had found to be the elevation of the Mountain House during last winter, so that this could not be the case. In addition, the change in the vegetation, especially the occurrence of cedar, convinced me that we were really on a branch of the Columbia.

I accordingly only followed it for two days, and on 29th reached the mouth of a large tributary, to N.W. This river is much larger than the Vermillion River, and about four times the size of the stream into which it flows, being about equal to the south branch at the point when we left it.

By this time, Hector had named the Brisco Range for Captain Arthur Brisco, a member of the 11th Hussars, who were immortalized in Alfred, Lord Tennyson's "The Charge of the Light Brigade." Brisco was also briefly attached to the Palliser Expedition. Hector named Mt. Vaux for his friend William Sandys Wright Vaux, who was for 29 years the resident antiquarian at the British Museum, one of Hector's favourite haunts. With the discovery of this major river, however, Hector's luck was about to change:

Here I received a severe kick in the chest from my horse, rendering me senseless, and disabling me for some time. My recovery might have been much more tedious than it was, but for the fact that we were now starving, and I found it absolutely necessary to push on after two days.

A more complete account of this accident was published in a later version of the complete Palliser Expedition papers, which include Hector's own journals used to write his October 9, 1859, report to the Secretary of State. It seems that one of the packhorses, tired of the continuous shin-bruising deadfall, had opted for easier travel by streambed. The date was August 29, 1858.

We had travelled a few miles when we came to a large flat, where the wide valley terminated, dividing into two branch valleys, one from the north-west and the other to the south-west. Here we met a very large stream, equal in size to Bow River where we crossed it. This river descends the valley from the north-west, and, on entering the wide valley of Beaverfoot River, turns back on its course at a sharp angle, receives that river as a tributary, and flows off to the south-west through the other valley. Just above the angle there is a fall about 40 feet in height, where the channel is contracted by perpendicular rocks.

A little way above this fall, one of our pack horses, to escape the fallen timber, plunged into the stream, luckily where it formed an eddy, but the banks were so steep that we had great difficulty in getting him out. In attempting to recatch my own horse, which had strayed off while we were engaged with the one in the water, he kicked me in the chest, but I had luckily got close to him before he struck out, so that I did not get the full force of the blow. However, it knocked me down and rendered me senseless for some time. This was unfortunate, as we had seen no tracks of game in the neighbourhood, and were now without food; but I was so hurt that we could not proceed further that day at least. My men covered me up under a tree, and I sent them all off to try and raise something to eat.

Hector does not mention that his men, having come to the conclusion that he had been killed by the blow, dug a grave for him. The horse had kicked him with both feet and quite knocked the wind from Hector's lungs. Hector later reminisced that he regained consciousness within moments of being buried alive. Since he had not yet recovered his speech, Hector had to wink an eye to prove to his saddened companions that he was still alive.

Hector's account is understated in a typically Victorian way. Circumstances were a lot worse than he lets on. The expedition's only doctor had received a life-threatening kick in the chest just at that point on the journey when starvation threatened the survival of the whole party. Although their situation was grim, Hector realized that a new pass over the Great Divide was awaiting him at the upper end of the valley through which this unmapped river flowed. Despite the injury, Hector had to keep the expedition's objectives clearly in mind. Hector had just entered into what is now Yoho National Park. His men were out looking for food and a way upvalley. Although he was seriously injured, he was still driven to continue his work. He still had to follow his Kicking Horse River to its source and cross the Great Divide back into what is now Alberta.

The following borrows from both his journal notes and the letter describing these events that Hector sent to England on October 9, 1858:

As I was quite unable to move, I sent my interpreter, Peter Erasmus, to ascend Mount Hunter, which is included in the angle of the Kicking Horse River. He ascended for 3,496 feet, and obtained a view, to the west, of snow-clad peaks as far as the eye can reach. Over the tops of Brisco's range, and all to the left of S.W., he could perceive no mountains, so that if that portion of country is occupied by any they must be of inferior altitude.

The men all returned at night without having killed anything. Nimrod had tracked some wapiti, but there were traces of Indians having been in the neighbourhood in spring, probably Shouswaps or Kootanies, and they found a very bad trail leading down the valley to the S.W. Nimrod, who had been that way, found the river soon became hemmed in by high rocks, so that the trail had to go high up over the mountain. There had only been two tents, with very

It was near Wapta Falls that James Hector was kicked by his horse, an event that resulted in the naming of the river. Wapta Falls is accessible from the Trans-Canada Highway by way of a short, well-graded trail.

few horses, and they appear to have returned from this part by the same road they came. At one of the camps he found wool of the mount [sic] goat, and also wapiti hair. The deer tracks he had seen were leading up the valley to the N.W., and were not fresh. This evening we saw several flocks of geese flying down the valley to the S.W.

Hector's account of the movement of Native peoples through this country gives clear evidence that these mountains were occupied, if only in summer, by vigorous, well-adapted groups of Native people who knew the geography of Yoho well enough to travel in it regularly. Popular newspaper stories and novels of the day were often based on personal accounts like those written by Hector, but the popular press did not always accurately portray the significance of Native contribution to North American exploration. By the next day, August 30, Hector had begun to recover:

was so much better by noon, that I took a meridian altitude.....The men were again hunting to-day, and Peter and Brown found a large flock of white goats, but the only one they shot managed to get to the edge of the precipice and fell over, so that they got none of the meat.

Nimrod went a long distance after the deer, and came back quite lame, having run a sharp spike into his foot. He had seen the wapiti and missed a fine buck. We were now in a bad way, as, although I had kept a private cache of about five pounds of pemmican, which I now produced, it was only enough for one meal for us all. I intended, however, to make it last for three days, by which time we should, from the look of the stream which I intended to ascend, be able to reach the height of land, and get back to the east slope of the mountains where we would be sure to find game.

Hector's observations of wildlife make interesting reading, especially in the context of what is known today about the habitats and distribution of Yoho's major mammals. Hector's description of the "wapiti" suggests that he his talking about the North American elk and not the whitetail or mule deer species that shares part of the same mountain habitat. It seems, from this account at least, that elk were not common in the Kicking Horse Valley at the time of the first European explorations. They are conspicuous today because they were re-introduced into the Canadian Rockies in the 1920s. Although cougars, or mountain lions, are exceedingly rare in Yoho today, Hector's account of his travels along the Beaverfoot indicate that they may have been common in Yoho a century ago. Since these graceful predators are at the top of the food chain, it may be that there was more game in the Kicking Horse and neighboring valleys than Hector imagined. How unearthly the sound of these big cats must have been in the darkness of the mountain night:

While traversing this valley, since coming on the Kootanie River, we have had no trail to follow, and it did not seem to have been frequented by Indians for many years. This makes the absence of game all the more extraordinary. The only animal which seemed to occur at all was the panther. The Indian saw one, and in the evenings we heard them calling, as they skirted round our camp, attracted by the scent.

Despite his injury, Hector somehow found the wherewithal to continue observing the nature of the forests in the area of the junction of the Beaverfoot and this new river they had come upon before his accident. The forest Hector describes is very different from today:

The timber along Beaver Foot River is mostly young, but there are the remains of what had been a noble growth of forests, consisting of cedar, pines, and spruce, among the latter of which is the magnificent prusche, which sometimes reaches four yards in circumference. I also saw a few young maples (Negundo fraso). Berries of many kinds were very abundant, and, indeed, had it not been for this we would have suffered much from hunger.

On the following day, August 31, Hector realized that the party could no longer remain at the junction of the Beaverfoot and this new river. If the party were to avoid starving to death, it had to continue upvalley. Although still very seriously injured, Hector had to mount his horse and join the party's slow advance into unknown country. Injured and starving, he nevertheless continued to give a complete account of the party's hardships in his journal:

Every morning just now we have dense fogs, that generally last until nine or ten o'clock, but the evenings are fine and clear. After travelling a mile along the left bank of the river from the N.W., which because of the accident the men had named Kicking Horse River, we crossed to the opposite side. It was 90 to 100 yards wide, and almost too deep to ford. The motion on horseback gave me great pain, but we managed to get along slowly till noon. We left the river a considerable distance to our right, following notched trees that Nimrod had marked the day before when out hunting in order to show us the best way, as an Indian soon finds out the right direction to carry a trail in.

At nightfall we again struck the river, where it passes through a narrow defile, and through which we found a well-marked trail. This is generally the case whenever the valleys are narrow, as there, whenever Indians have passed in former times, they have been limited to the same track; while in wider parts of the valley they hunt about in search of game, without leaving distinct traces of where they pass.

The deposits of red and grey sand, with clay and gravel, are at least 600 feet thick in the valley. Our course had changed almost to due north, and we passed over the grey slate strata, dipping first to the N.E. at 5 degrees, and then changing to a high angle in the same direction. Where we encamped the river is hemmed by high precipices of blue limestone. The river is very muddy, and with the imperfect tackle we have, consisting of some large cod hooks and twine, we cannot catch any trout.

It had now been three days since the accident. Progress up the valley of the Kicking Horse was painfully slow. Hector was mending but still suffering greatly. The entire party was fearful of starvation. On September 1, 1858, the exhausted members of the expedition continued upvalley past what surveyor George Dawson later called Otterhead Creek and the Ottertail River. Following the river, the party advanced toward the junction of the Amiskwi and Kicking Horse rivers. Between the present-day town of Field and the mouth of the Amiskwi River, the Kicking Horse makes a sharp turn from a northeast to an east-west course, creating the angle that Hector cut across. The canyon Hector describes is where, today, visitors stop by the thousands to view the Natural Bridge, another of Yoho's famous natural wonders.

*S*tarted early, sending Nimrod and Peter ahead to hunt. The valley soon after starting got very wide, with extensive swampy flats and clumps of fine timber. The willows fringing the margins of these grassy swamps exactly resembled hedgerows enclosing green fields.

Halt at noon ....a little way below where the river receives two large tributaries, one from the east and the other from the N.W.

Above this point the main stream makes a large bend to the east, to avoid which we crossed a high rocky spur of the mountain, and again met the river by descending into a magnificent canyon, where we encamped.

It is hard to sleep when you are starving. The expedition rose early on the morning of September 2, knowing that travel would be slow work for the tired, hungry horses. The party advanced along the outwash plain of the Kicking

Horse River, past the present site of Field, and began the ascent of the steep western side of Kicking Horse Pass about where the Trans-Canada Highway is today. After cresting the summit, the explorers passed what are now called Sink Lake and Summit or Wapta Lake and crossed the divide into what is now Alberta.

Started very early, as our only hope of getting any game was by reaching the east side of the mountain. Nimrod had indeed again seen wapiti yesterday, but the fallen woods were so difficult to hunt in, that with his lame foot he only got a long shot, which he missed. We travelled on the shingle flat, which occupies the full width of the valley, crossing and recrossing the river, which must during the spring floods cover the whole valley bottom. After five miles the valley terminated in a sudden slope, covered with heavy pine forests. Entering these we began to ascend rapidly, but loitered a good deal to eat large blueberries, that grew in abundance, and which we were very glad to get, although not very substantial food, when we had been fasting altogether for the past day, and living on only very short allowance for the previous five. After gaining a considerable height, we found it necessary to cross the stream, which was boiling and leaping through a narrow channel of pink quartzose rock. It was with much difficulty that we effected a crossing, and then we had much climbing over moss-covered rocks, our horses often sliding and falling. One, an old grey, that was always more clumsy than the others, lost his balance in passing along a ledge, which overhung a precipitous slope about 150 feet in height, and down he went, luckily catching sometimes on the trees; at last he came to a temporary pause by falling right on his back, the pack acting as a fender; however, in his endeavours to get up he started down hill again, and at last slid on a dead tree that stuck out at right angles to the slope, balancing himself with his legs dangling on either side of the trunk of the tree in a most comical manner. It was only by making a round of a mile that we succeeded in

The Natural Bridge is a stone arch across the Kicking Horse River just west of Field. It was first described by James Hector.

getting him back, all battered and bruised, to the rest of the horses. In the lower part of the ascent we passed much cedar and birch, but as we rose we got into forests exclusively composed of spruce fir. We travelled eight hours before camping, the last two being over fine level ground through open forest. We passed many small lakes, and at last reached a small stream flowing to the east, and were again on the Saskatchewan slope of the mountains. The large stream we had been ascending takes its rise from a glacier to the east of the valley through which we had passed. We encamped in a beautiful spot beside a lake, with excellent pasture for the horses. I had killed a grouse, and we were glad to boil it up with some ends of candles and odd pieces of grease, to make something like a supper for the five of us after a very hard day's work. We were now 1,275 feet above our encampment of last night, and the cold was very sharp, and we felt it more severely in our famished state.

Although Hector and his party had passed out of Yoho, they were not out of the woods yet. On September 3, Hector crossed Bath Creek and then the Bow River. Very much to the good fortune of their clumsy grey packhorse, their forced fast was about to come to an end:

This morning all the swamps were covered with ice. As I was now nearly recovered from the accident, I started with Nimrod at daylight to hunt, leaving the men and horses to follow a prescribed course to the east. We took our horses with us, and after a few miles we came to a large stream from the west, up the valley of which we saw a great glacier. Following it down, we came after five miles to a large river, which Nimrod at once recognized as Bow River, and then I began to recognize the mountains down the valley, 15 or 20 miles to the east, as the Castle Mountains. The descent from our camp at the height of land of the pass which we had just traversed is very slight to the Bow River, and cannot amount to more than 100 feet. We crossed Bow River, and leaving our horses tethered in a swamp, set off to hunt on foot. We saw several fresh moose tracks, and followed one for more than two hours, but failing to come up with it. Towards noon, on coming to the river, I found our party had crossed, so I made for them in order to get the latitude. Nimrod soon started again into the woods, and had not been long gone, when we heard most furious firing, and in a short time he returned in a high state of glee, having shot a moose. We at once moved our camp to where it lay, about one mile distant, in a thicket of willows. It was a doe, and very lean, but, notwithstanding, we soon set about cooking and eating to make up for our long fast. It was not till we got the food that we all found out how depressed and weak we were, as desperation had been keeping us up. I had three days before promised that if nothing was killed by to-day I would kill one of the horses, and this evening, if Nimrod had not killed the moose, the old grey that fell over the cliff would have been sacrificed. I had refrained from killing a horse sooner, as I have been warned by experi-

enced travellers that once the first horse is killed for food many more are sure to follow, as the flesh of a horse out of condition is so inferior as merely to create a craving for large quantities of it, without giving strength or vigour to induce the hunters to exert themselves to kill other game. The prospect of starving is then looked upon with indifference, as they know it will be avoided by killing another horse, until at last too few are left to carry the necessities for the party, who then undergo great sufferings, and, as in the case of several American expeditions, some may even perish.

The next morning, a Stoney suddenly appeared in Hector's camp. Drawn from kilometers away by the smell of a cook fire, he announced that his party was camped down-valley. Since the weather continued stormy and cold, Hector's party joined the Stoneys, who gave Hector further lessons on how to dry moose meat so that it would not spoil.

Achievements of the Palliser Expedition

So ended the first scientific exploration by Europeans into the region now known as Yoho. Delighted that he had discovered a major new pass in the Rockies, Hector then worked his way north along the Great Divide. Searching every valley for a new pass, he gradually made his way to Fort Edmonton, following roughly the same route as the Icefields Parkway to Saskatchewan River Crossing and then following the Saskatchewan to Rocky Mountain House.

The Palliser Expedition identified eight passes for the consideration of the Secretary of State in England. These included Cow Dung Lake Portage or "Leather Pass," now known as the Yellowhead Pass, west of Jasper Boat Encampment on the original Athabasca Portage; Howse Pass; Kicking Horse Pass; Vermilion Pass; Kananaskis or Emigrant Pass; Crow Nest Pass, now called Crowsnest Pass; and Kootenay Pass. Given the undeveloped state of the Atlantic and Pacific colonies in Canada, the expedition did not, at this time at least, recommend building a wagon road through the difficult and dangerous terrain of the Canadian West. Instead, the final pages of the lengthy Palliser report to Parliament recommended that the British government consider an international undertaking with American railroads planning to use a "North Pacific route." "A route laid close to the international boundary," the report concluded, "could most easily be carried over British ground." Many people in powerful positions in Canada would later disagree with this assumption. Fortunately for Canadians today, their disagreement would spawn a nation.

The Palliser report subsequently fell into the hands of politicians. Many argued that the expedition added little to what had already been detailed through the explorations of David Thompson. This argument by no means suggests that the expedition was unsuccessful. Captain Palliser and his men were able to explore and describe a great deal of the geography, geology, botany, and

Though James Hector and his party were starving when they reached the summit of Kicking Horse Pass from the west, they did not fail to comment on the beauty of that area of the Great Divide.

climate of the north-central part of the continent. That part of the expedition under James Hector was also credited with the first formal maps and written descriptions of Yoho.

But Hector's ultimate accomplishment is much greater than this. Hector's significance to the history is not that he was the first to explore the heart of what is now the park. Native peoples had already made extensive inquiries into the wonder of Yoho and knew its valleys reasonably well. Nor was Hector particularly important because he was the first European to visit the area. It is entirely possible that a fur-trader or wanderer or two had occasionally made his way into Yoho before Hector's wide-ranging exploration of the Great Divide. Nor was Hector important because he explored a great deal of Yoho. His explorations only examined the main valley of the Kicking Horse River.

Hector is important to Yoho and to the Canadian Rockies because he brought different interests to the West. He was not a fur-trader, a missionary, a prospector, or a soldier of fortune of any kind. He was the first of a new breed of traveller whose expectations were fashioned by aesthetics as well as the pursuit of easy wealth. The perception of the once-barren wasteland of peaks that composed the Canadian West was about to be changed. Hector replaced a landscape of terror and fear with mountains of imagination. The published accounts of the expedition told of a new kind of West that nurtured freedom of the spirit and provided room for that spirit to wander in. Hector imposed a new geography on the Rockies, a geography not of limitation but of possibility. His accounts told of an entire landscape history waiting to be experienced and described. A whole new world of knowledge was waiting for those with the energy and the curiosity to explore it.

The map that Hector took home was a map of wonder. Alhough Hector did not see it at the time, Canada was about to become blue mountains, Mounties, and moonlit ice — and the Canadian Pacific Railway would put Yoho, with all its wonders, right in the middle of it.

A train negotiates through the spiral tunnel section of the Field Hill. Mt. Stephen provides the backdrop.

Chapter 2

....

Surveying the Wonder

ative peoples were the first human cultures in what is now Yoho. It is amply clear from early accounts that Native groups visited the valley of the Kicking Horse River and its tributaries only seasonally. Used principally as a summer hunting ground, this high, wild country was simply too severe to survive in during the winter. Three Native groups appear to have visited the area. The Shuswap Indians travelled widely along the western edge of the Great Divide, as did the Kootenays. Both of these groups, as David Thompson indicates in his journals from the early 19th century, appear to have made regular spring and summer journeys over various passes into what is now Alberta. A variety of Plains Natives made visits to the major valleys of the east side of the Great Divide in summer to hunt and to cut lodgepole pine trees, out of which they fashioned teepee poles. These groups, which include the Assiniboines, or the Stoneys as they are now called, crossed some of the major passes along the Great Divide from the east. In their explorations, they often wandered into the peripheral hunting territories of British Columbia's mountain Natives. These crossings were reduced after European contact because warfare between groups on either side of the divide had become more frequent and more fierce as a result of the introduction of horses and guns.

All the early first-hand accounts of exploration in the Canadian West give at least some credit to Native peoples who showed Europeans the way through country that was new to them and demonstrated to them how to survive in it. Later, armchair historians encouraged the notion that European explorers actually "discovered" these places. Only very simplistic histories of the Canadian West can attribute actual discovery to visiting Europeans. Native peoples preceded Europeans in the Rockies by thousands of years and knew the country intimately.

The Second Generation of Europeans

The first generation of explorers in the Canadian Rockies was succeeded by railway surveyors, engineers, and thousands of usually poorly educated labourers from all over the world. They worked hard, drank hard when they could, and occasionally left their bones in the beds over which the tracks were

31

laid. When they were no longer needed, most of them moved on. Few were interested in the culture of the local peoples who seemed to be retreating just beyond the rails as the railway workers advanced westward. For most of these Europeans, the history of the Rockies began when they arrived.

With the coming of this second generation of Europeans, transformation exploded upon Canada's mountain West. More cultural change took place in 25 years than had occurred since the glaciers of the last ice age had come and gone. Primeval valleys shuddered with the dull roar of exploding dynamite. The ringing of the hammers on cold steel drowned out the gurgle of stream water, and the silence of the valleys, inhabited for centuries only by rocks, trees, and wildlife, was broken by the eerie whistle of the steam train. In the noise, the confusion, and the politics, Native peoples were forgotten.

The Palliser Expedition's report to the Secretary of State for the colonies examined potential transportation routes across the western half of British North America. Although it did not eagerly support the development of so much as a wagon road, the report did stimulate lively debate about the future of the Canadian West. Much was made of real and imagined American threats to the political sovereignty of these lightly populated lands. A nationalist movement began to grow in Canada. Confederation debates demanded a reassessment of the relationship of the West to the political and economic will of a developing national identity. Two years after the confederation of Canada's upper and maritime provinces, the continent's first national railway was completed in the United States. Although Canada had a tenth of the population of its southern neighbor, the Canadian government decided that if the United States could afford a national railway, it could too. This sounds a little like an impetuous 18-year-old claiming he is going to buy a Rolls-Royce and use his weekly allowance to make the payments, but that is pretty much what happened. The building of Canada's national railway was as much an astonishing political coup as it was a feat of extraordinary engineering finesse. The financing of this rather insane scheme was a good trick also.

Canada at Confederation was a disjointed country to say the least. Just as now, settlement was concentrated in Upper Canada in Ontario and Quebec, which was the country's centre of discourse with Europe and the eastern United States. The only other large concentration of people was along the Pacific coast, which was the country's centre of discourse with Asia and the American West. To achieve greatness, Central Canada had to embrace the west coast by way of the almost limitless lands that formed the interior of the continent. Four years after Confederation, the Dominion of Canada made a rash proposal to the Colony of British Columbia, offering the colony a railway in exchange for political union. The proposal did not need the legal-sounding language and all the capital letters that were put into it to make it sound like a substantial offer:

*The Government of the Dominion undertakes to secure the commence-
ment simultaneously, within two years from the date of the Union, of the construction of a Railway from the Pacific towards the Rocky Mountains, towards
such a point as may be selected and from such point as may be selected, East of
the Rocky Mountains, towards the Pacific, to connect the Seaboard of British
Columbia with the Railway system of Canada; and further, to secure the completion of such Railway within ten years from the date of Union.....*

The builders of Canada's national railway knew where they wanted to go,
but they didn't know what lay between them and their goal. Duly, In April of
1871, an engineer named Sandford Fleming was hired to solve the problem of
locating the railway over its nearly 6000 kilometre route across Canada. An
army of surveyors fanned out over the country to determine the lay of the land.
The mountain West was immediately identifies as posing a special problem for
those looking for a railway route, so a number of very proficient surveyors were
assigned to the Rockies. Since Kicking Horse Pass had already been noted and
mapped by James Hector, surveying efforts by Walter Moberly and others were
concentrated on other sections of the Great Divide. The efforts of the surveyors,
however, were brought up short by a scandal in 1873 that led to the fall of the
country's Conservative government under John A. Macdonald. Once in power,
the Liberals, under Alexander Mackenzie, put a temporary halt to Canada's
railway madness.

Surveying in Western Canada continued sporadically throughout the next
five years. During that time, British Columbia became restless over the
Dominion's lack of progress toward the fulfilment of its promise and threatened
to leave the Confederation. A recession also showered cold water on the
nation's enthusiasm for unity. By 1878, however, Macdonald's Conservatives
were back in power and the dream of a railway once again gathered steam. A
new railway syndicate was established, arguments over where the Pacific ter-
minus would be located were finally resolved, and as the railway began to
snake westward from Montreal, contracts were let to begin laying the rails from
the Pacific inland toward the Great Divide. It did not seem to matter that a
route across the prairies and through the Rockies had yet to be firmly chosen;
the Great Railway had finally been started and the rest would take care of itself.

Uncertainty over which pass the railway should use in the Rockies was
complicated by a number of factors. Although Yellowhead Pass was the pre-
ferred route of Sir Sandford Fleming, it was argued that a line that far north of
the international border would require more trackage and would therefore be
more expensive to build. At this same time, findings by the respected botanist
John Macoun were temporarily demolishing Palliser's earlier reports that the
southern prairies were mere deserts. A more southerly route would not only

cost less but might also open up the Canadian prairies for agricultural development. When the decision was made to lay the track in the south, two obstacles remained. No known route existed through the Selkirks, and an acceptable pass through the Rockies had yet to be identified. The responsibility of solving these two problems was given to an American engineer named Albert Bowman Rogers. A. B. Rogers was tough, miserable, and mean and could swear the bluest streak of profanities in the Rockies. But he was absolutely committed to the task. It was through Rogers that the railway ultimately found its way through Kicking Horse Pass to Yoho.

The Bishop of Blue Thunder

Major A. B. Rogers was born in Orleans, Massachusetts, on May 28, 1829. A Yale graduate, Rogers quickly developed a reputation as an outrageous character and one of the best railway and civil engineers on the continent. While working on the Erie Canal, the Chicago, Milwaukee and St. Paul, and a number of other, lesser railway projects, Rogers became a grand master of most of the obscenities in the English language. By the time he went to work for the Canadian Pacific in 1880, Rogers was already well-known by the nickname of "the Bishop." He also possessed a respected reputation for almost superhuman physical endurance.

Major Albert Bowman Rogers was a legend among railway engineers. He could swear, ride and starve better than any other man in Canadian railway history. His unflagging persistence resulted in Kicking Horse Pass being chosen as the rail route over the Great Divide. (Photo courtesy of the Whyte Museum of the Canadian Rockies.)

Many of Rogers's explorations followed up on leads on potential routes left behind by earlier surveying parties. Following an eagle up a remote valley on the western edge of the Selkirk Mountains in 1865, Walter Moberly had discovered Eagle Pass. In the spring of 1881, Rogers advanced past Eagle Pass to the head of the valley and, by way of a fork that Moberly had not visited, discovered the glacial headwaters of the Illecillewaet River. At the headwaters of the Illecillewaet, Rogers was certain he had found the pass through the Selkirks that was the key to southern route of the railway. Now that Rogers Pass had been discovered, it would not take long to pick a logical route through the Rockies, the next and last mountain obstacle in British Columbia. But Rogers had only travelled to one side of his pass and did not know what its 29 kilometer descent would be like. Rogers charged himself with further investigation and rushed back to the Rockies to organize the tracing of the rail route east from the Great Plains to the Great Divide and over Kicking Horse Pass, which had scarcely been examined since James Hector last saw it in September of 1858. In so doing, the Bishop would come into contact with a man who could see past his gruff and miserable facade and to the sincerity and kindness that were at the centre of Rogers's being. That man was Tom Wilson. This quiet cowboy would put the next grand human stamp on Yoho.

Until he took his discharge to work on the railway in the spring of 1881, Tom Wilson was an officer in the service of the North-West Mounted Police at Fort Walsh in the Northwest Territory. Thinking a change of career would suit him, Wilson hired on at Fort Benton, Montana, to assist in surveying a route through the Rockies. He later found himself hired on as a packer by P. K. Hyndman, Chief Engineer for Major A. B. Rogers, Engineer-in-Charge of the Mountain Section of the Canadian Pacific Railway.

On July 5, 1881, Wilson departed Fort Calgary as part of a large movement of supplies, including 80 packhorses to freight supplies into the mountains. The party was to await Major Rogers on the Bow River at the entrance to the Rockies. Wilson did not have to wait long to meet the great engineer, and when he met him, he understood immediately what kind of work it was going to take to make this railway plan work. Tom Wilson did not leave behind extensive journals. What he wrote about A. B. Rogers, however, is pure Canadiana. His accounts also tell us that travel in Yoho had not become any safer since James Hector had travelled there 23 years before. This quote and all others by Wilson in this book are from Trail Blazer of the Canadian Rockies, the published account of Tom Wilson's life as he told it to W. E. Round, published by the Glenbow-Alberta Institute, Calgary, 1972. Many years after the fact, here is Wilson's description of how he and Rogers met:

On the 15th of July I had strolled a short distance west of the camp and was sitting smoking alongside the narrow Indian trail when suddenly a mottled roan cayuse, carrying a rider, appeared round a curve. Behind it came two packhorses then two other animals ridden by Shuswap Indians. The leader, whom I instantly sensed was Major Rogers, wore an old white helmet and a brown canvas suit. His condition, well, dirty doesn't begin to describe it.

His voluminous sideburns waved like flags in a breeze; his piercing eyes seemed to look at and see through everything at once. I had heard that Major Rogers was famous for his tobacco chewing ability and may have doubted the stories I had heard. Such doubts, if I had any, were dispelled during the first few minutes I was with him. Every few minutes a stream of tobacco juice erupted from between his sideburns; I'll bet there were not many trees along-side the trail that had escaped his deadly tobacco juice aim.

Someone once said of him, "Give Rogers six plugs of chewing tobacco and five bacon rinds, and he will travel for two weeks". The man who said that was no exaggerator. Despite his fifty-odd years he leapt from his horse in a manner that many a younger man could have envied.....

We learned later that Major Rogers, accompanied by his twenty-one year old nephew, A. L. Rogers, better known as Al, had travelled from St. Paul to Kamloops, B.C. where the Hudson's Bay Company had a trading post. After some trouble he had secured the services of ten strapping young Indians. The contract he made with them is unique in history. By its terms, if any of them returned home without letters of good report to the mission priest, then their wages would be forfeited to the Church and their Chief Louie would lay one hundred lashes on the back of each offender. They agreed to serve Major Rogers without grumbling.

After great hardships Major Rogers had not been successful in his attempt to cross the Selkirks by ascending the western slope, but he had seen enough to make him confident that it could be done. He had been obliged, though scarcity of food, to retrace his steps to the Columbia and travel down that stream to Fort Colville, Washington Territory.

Rogers's unrelenting journey from Fort Colville to the east side of the Rockies is further evidence of how hard he was prepared to drive himself and everyone in his service toward the goal of surveying a final rail route. Rogers sped from Fort Colville to Spokane, where he secured packhorses, and from there crossed Pen d'Oreille Pass in northern Idaho, crossed the Kootenay at Bonner's Ferry, and followed an old trail up the Moyie River to Wild Horse mining camp, later known as Fort Steele. After hiring two Shuswaps to accompany him, Rogers followed the Columbia to near where Windermere is today, crossed the Brisco Range, followed the Cross River to the summit of Whiteman's Pass, then dropped into the Bow Valley about where the town of Canmore is today. At Wild Horse camp, Rogers had made arrangements for his nephew to begin exploration of Kicking Horse Pass from the west while he rounded the mountains to begin an assault from the east. Rogers's railway map was gradually coming together. Wilson describes his part in the Kicking Horse Pass expedition, and in so doing perpetuates the myth that Rogers, and not James Hector, was the first to pass through Yoho. The account tells us more about native travel in Yoho:

He [Rogers] had left his nephew to take the packtrain from Wild Horse camp to the mouth of the Kicking Horse River and up that stream to the Great Divide, a feat never accomplished before not even by Indians. The redskins had a trail up the Kicking Horse as far as the Ottertail but beyond that

*they never used the Kicking Horse Valley. Their route lay up the Ottertail,
over McArthur Pass and then down to the Divide. The Kicking Horse Pass
was too difficult for horses to travel, so the natives never used it.*

The party worked its way slowly up the Bow River Valley toward the Great
Divide. In his gruff way, Rogers was living up to his reputation. The men were
already complaining. Only Tom Wilson sympathized with Rogers:

*Cutting and widening the Indian trail, we worked our way westward
until at noon of the third day we halted near the base of the mountain known
as Hole-In-The-Wall, directly opposite the Simpson Pass. There Major Rogers
gave us another talk, told us that he intended visiting every camp while the
work was on and that he also intended doing a certain amount of exploring. He
then called for a volunteer to accompany him and act as his special attendant.*

*Silence greeted his request; there were good reasons for it. Every man pre-
sent had learned in three days to hate the Major with a real hatred. He had no
mercy on horses or men; he had none on himself. The labourers hated him for
the way he drove them and the packers for the way he abused the horses; he
never gave their needs a thought. When no one volunteered I thought I might
as well take a chance and so took him up.*

This invitation from Rogers was, in fact, an invitation to become part of history. There were a good dozen other men there who could have easily decided
to participate in the discovery of many of the most significant natural features
in the Rockies, but they simply hated Rogers too much to do so. One of these
was A. E. Tregent, who, in a letter to Wilson dated June 4, 1929, recalled the
fateful day when Wilson signed on with the Bishop. Tregent was perfectly cor-
rect in his assessment of the hazards: "I well remember the day that you took on
Major Rogers. You were the only man that would go with that old geyser.
Nobody else had the pluck to run the chance of being starved to death or lost in
the woods."

All his life, Wilson did his best to improve the image of Major Rogers. His
account of what happened next is an example of how much Wilson respected
the old man. Rogers and Wilson have travelled up the Bow to where its tributaries flow into it from the eastern slopes of Kicking Horse Pass. Rogers has sent
his nephew on an almost impossible mission and is concerned about his safety:

*We followed the creek until evening then camped. About mid-after-
noon of the next day we reached the east end of what we at once called Kicking
Horse Lake and pitched camp. This lake is now known as Lake Wapta. We had
barely finished pitching the tents when Major Rogers rode in. "Has that
damned little cuss Al got here yet?" was his first question. We were to learn
later that a sincere affection existed between uncle and nephew and that the*

Tom Wilson disliked Albert Rogers when he first met him but gradually grew to respect his courage and dedication to the task of completing the country's first trans-continental rail line. (Photo courtesy of the Whyte Museum of the Canadian Rockies.)

former's manner of speaking about Al was an armour, a mask that hid the Major's true feelings. He wore a thick mask and it was in later being able to see beneath it that my dislike for him changed to affection.

    Very few men have ever learned to understand him, yet he had a generous heart and real affection for many. He cultivated a gruff manner to conceal the emotions that he seemed ashamed to let anyone else sense. His driving ambition was to have his name handed down in history; for that he faced unknown dangers and suffered privations. To have the key pass of the Selkirks bear his name was the ambition he fought to realise.....

    As soon as the Major discovered that Al had not arrived he went on the rampage. How he pranced about! "Where has that damn little cuss got to?" he asked repeatedly. "If anything happens to that damn little cuss I'll never show my face in St. Paul again," he informed the gang, the mountains, and the whole of nature. That he had given that "damn little cuss", a twenty-one year old youth, the immense task of being the first white man to travel the whole length of the Kicking Horse meant nothing to him. He had given Al the job and expected him to accomplish it although it meant doing what the Indians refused to do, travel the Kicking Horse Gorge.

Wilson's suggestion that James Hector had not travelled the length of the Kicking Horse is true. Hector had come upon the Kicking Horse River by way of the Beaverfoot. He had missed the section of the river between Wapta Falls and the Columbia, where it enters Kicking Horse Canyon, a long, deep, sunless gorge where even Natives refused to travel. In addition to Hector's route, Rogers's nephew was expected to explore this section as part of the potential route of the rail line. Despite his oaths, Rogers was rightly concerned about the well-being of that "damn little cuss" Albert:

Suddenly he conceived the idea that as we had reached the summit behind schedule then Albert might have gone on east along the south side of the Bow. He yelled at me to get the horses ready and in a few minutes we were headed eastwards. It was a very hot day and the glaciers were pouring torrents into the streams. On reaching the creek we found it terribly swollen, and to make matters worse the current raced around numerous large boulders. All streams that run direct from glaciers begin to rise in the afternoon and subside in the early morning. Knowing this, I halted at the creek and suggested to the Major that it would be advisable to camp for the night and cross the stream when the water would be lower and less dangerous. He shot one of his famous "Blue _ _ _" oaths at me. "Afraid of it are you? Want the old man to show you how to ford it?" It all happened in half a minute; he spurred his horse in, the current took its legs from under it, the Major disappeared in the foaming, silt-laden water, and the horse rolled downstream.

I grabbed a long pole and managed to push it towards the Major; he seized it and I hauled him ashore. The horse struggled to its feet and climbed out a little way below us. Once ashore, the old man, for so I had begun to think of him, gave me a funny look. "Blue _ _ _", he remarked, "Light a fire and then get that damned horse. Blue _ _ _, it's cold." Needless to say we camped there the night and crossed the stream the next morning.

This incident gave Bath Creek its name....Bath Creek flows directly from Daly Glacier, therefore there are many times when the Bow, before its junction with Bath Creek, is running clear; then the latter pours its torrent of silty water into the larger stream and discolours it for miles downstream. Whenever this occurred the men of our gang would remark, "Hello, the old man's taking another bath", hence the name.

The good soaking in the meltwater of Yoho's Daly glacier improved the Major's appearance slightly, but it did not help him find his nephew, who was still foundering around the Kicking Horse Valley. Rogers was beginning to panic. The next morning Rogers and Wilson headed eastward on the other side of the Bow looking for Albert and met another party of surveyors, who upon questioning reported they had not seen Albert either. This party joined Rogers and Wilson and returned to their camp at the summit of Kicking Horse Pass:

On arrival there we found that Al was still missing so the old man, became more excited. He wanted every man to turn out and search for Al in the pitch black darkness. The men refused; they had good reason to. They did not know the country and believed it held terrible dangers.

How the Major put in the night I do not know, but at daybreak he was on the warpath cursing about late risers. He sent some of the men up what is now known as Cataract Creek and others in different directions. All had explicit orders about firing revolvers and lighting signal fires when the lost one was found.

Fred Palling and I were given light packs and revolvers, and sent down the south side of the Kicking Horse where there were game trails but no Indian trails. We had to go on foot and what a trip it was. On account of the high canyon walls we were forced to keep well up the mountain side. We toiled through thick timber where we could not see a yard ahead; we trod warily on stretches of deep deceptive moss that in places hid dangerous crevices and holes; we traversed rock and gravel slides that needed but a slight movement to start them rolling; and we scrambled over huge boulders, where one pushed the other up, then was in turn pulled up. We had no axe with us as the orders were to travel light.

It took us all day, a day of heavy toil, to reach the flats below where the stream, known today as the Yoho, joins the Kicking Horse. Thoroughly tired out we decided to spend the night on the flat. We had no tent; just a blanket each, some tea, bannock and boiled salt pork of the variety commonly known as sowbelly. A small tin pail was our only cooking utensil.

Following our meal we were lying smoking alongside the fire when from down the valley came a very faint report. It sounded like a pistol shot but neither of us could definitely say that it was. We decided to investigate, so started downstream in a hurry. We yelled as we ran then heard an answering shout. As we rounded a curve we almost fell on a man who was sitting by a small fire. It was Al Rogers. Starvation, mental and physical strain were clearly written on his face. He was very weak; for two days he had lived on a small porcupine and had eaten everything but the quills. He had left one Indian to guard the pack train at the mouth of the Kicking Horse and with the other Indian had started the upstream trek on foot.

From this second recorded report of Yoho, it appears that the country was impossibly difficult to travel in. The two European parties that travelled through the valley of the Kicking Horse had both suffered from starvation and acute exhaustion. It can easily be asked how a place like this received a name like Yoho unless that exclamation of awe really meant, "Wow, I lived through that." Rogers's theory was that any time you went through new country for the first time it was bound to be a little taxing.

After affectionately swearing at his nephew for a while, Rogers resumed his task of surveying Kicking Horse Pass. Two days later young Albert, having recovered somewhat from this epic Kicking Horse River adventure, joined a party of surveyors running a preliminary line down the pass. Wilson and another packer headed up the Bow Valley for more supplies. Upon returning, Wilson became Major Rogers's personal assistant. The relationship was terminated abruptly, perhaps not unexpectedly, when an argument erupted over where the two should camp one night. Wilson later resigned from the service of Major Rogers and went to Fort Macleod. Their partnership, however, was far from finished, as Wilson clearly remembered in his memoirs:

> As we shook hands at parting Major Rogers said, "Tom, you'll be sorry you're leaving me. I want you to be with me; you may not think you're coming back but you'll be here next year and I'll be looking for you." As I rode away I said to myself "He'll look a long time" but the old Major knew me better than I knew myself.

Wilson did not miss a thing in leaving. Rogers kept three of his surveying crews in the mountains until the end of October. He sent one of the gangs to Wild Horse camp by way of Crowsnest Pass so that the members of the gang could winter in the area and thus be prepared to enter the Kicking Horse from the west as soon as the snow started to melt in the spring of 1882. So it was that much of the surveying work in the Kicking Horse was already done when, true to Rogers's prediction, Wilson came back to work the following May.

When Wilson reported for work at Fort Benton, he met a small, dynamic man named M. F. Hurd, Rogers's new second-in-command. One of the most experienced railway engineers in the United States, Hurd was similar in some ways to Major Rogers. As Wilson observed, Hurd was a prodigious tobacco chewer and a hard worker who quickly gained the respect of the men who reported to him. Wilson liked him enough to later have Mt. Hurd in Yoho named for him.

Tom Wilson Finds Emerald Lake

For Wilson, the summer of 1882 began in much the same way the previous summer had begun. He began ferrying loads of equipment and supplies from Padmore, now called Kananaskis, to Rogers's main surveying camp at the summit of Kicking Horse Pass. While returning from his second trip for supplies,

Though popular history features Tom Wilson discovering Emerald Lake, it was really his horses that made the discovery. Wilson had purchased his stock from local natives who had visited the lake often enough that the horses knew the way there.

Wilson camped at the junction of the Pipestone River and the Bow. The next day, a small band of Stoneys camped at the same site. It was raining and soon everyone was gathered around a big fire. In the mist they heard the thunder of avalanches falling from above. One of the Stoneys in the party, a man whose tribe had given him a name that meant "money seeker" or "gold seeker", indicated to Wilson that the thunder was coming from "snow mountains above the lake of the little fishes." The following morning, Wilson invited the man, who also had the English name Edwin Hunter, to take him to the lake. They had little trouble reaching the lake by horse. Wilson named the stunning sheet of water Emerald Lake, and it appeared as such on the first geological map made of the area, drawn by George Dawson. Before the map was published in 1886, however, the Geographical Society of Canada had changed the name to Lake Louise in honour of Princess Louise Caroline Alberta, the fourth daughter of Queen Victoria. By the time Dawson's map was published, though, Wilson had already found another Emerald Lake in Yoho.

The day after first visiting Lake Louise, Wilson ran into Major Rogers, who, as Wilson's story goes at least, made a prophetic announcement about Wilson's future in the mountains: " 'Blue _ _ _', he roared, ' I knew you'd be back. I knew you'd be back. You'll never leave these mountains again as long as you live. They've got you now.' "

It did not take long for Rogers to confide to Wilson his growing doubts about what route the railway should take through the Rockies. Rogers was now more certain than ever that Rogers Pass was the right route through the Selkirks, but he did not know whether Howse Pass or Kicking Horse Pass was the most economical route over the Great Divide. Rogers wanted more information about the Howse area and offered Wilson a $50 bonus if he would go to Howse Pass to get it. Since a lone, lightly equipped traveller could move with the greatest speed, Wilson agreed to go alone and on foot.

Although the going was harder than Rogers had predicted, Wilson encountered few problems on his journey up the Bow River and down the north side of Bow Pass to the Saskatchewan River and the mouth of the Howse. Wilson got lost a few times on the ascent of Howse Pass from the east, but his problems did not really begin until he reached the summit and began his descent from the Great Divide into the valley of the Blaeberry River. The deadfall was nearly 3 metres deep and his progress slow and exhausting. Rogers had predicted that the journey would be brief, so this lone traveller had only carried food for 10 days. By the time Wilson reached the Blaeberry, he was starving. He soon became so weakened that he doubted he could make it to the confluence of the Blaeberry and the Columbia, where Rogers had agreed to meet him. At just the point when Wilson had decided to leave behind everything but his axe in an all-out attempt to make it to the Columbia, he heard voices and stumbled through the heavy darkness toward them. Suddenly the forest opened up and he saw a big campfire with two men silhouetted against the flames. Although Rogers barely showed it, he was fearfully worried about Wilson, and it was this that made them friends for the rest of their lives:

T*he Major looked at me for a moment — a queer look it was — then, "Blue _ _ _! What kept you so long?" he snorted and turned on his heel. Not another word did he speak until I had eaten and, with the two men, fetched my equipment from the bush and put out the fire I had left. On the way to do that they told me how for hours the Major had paced up and down like a caged lion, his oft repeated cry being "If that boy don't show up what in hell will I do? No one but a fool would send a lad on such a trip alone, and no one but a fool would try to make it alone.*

The next day Wilson gave Rogers a full report on the difficulties of Howse Pass, which seemed to satisfy the Major that Kicking Horse Pass was the right route after all. Wilson returned to the main camp at the summit of Kicking Horse Pass and resumed his task of packing supplies into Yoho for the survey crews. On one of his many trips down the pass into the main valley of the Kicking Horse, something happened to Wilson that in retrospect almost seems like a reward for the punishing journey he made up Howse Pass. After discovering Lake Louise a few weeks before, Wilson next found the real Emerald Lake — with the help of his horses:

On nearly each trip some of the horses would get sore backs or lacerated legs from sharp ledges or bad stumps, and the animals of poor stamina would show the effects of hard work. Expecting this to happen, we had about twice as many horses with us as were needed at one time. The extra ones, termed the hospital bunch, were turned out to graze in a slough at the foot of the big hill of the Kicking Horse Pass. Driving them down there was a safety measure for they had all come from the east, and some from only as far away as Morley; there was a chance that, if turned out east of the camp, they could wander home.

At the conclusion of one trip I decided to rest some of the horses I had been using and so I drove them to the pasture with the intention of bringing relief ones to the camp. At the very end of the "nose" of Mount Stephen my attention was arrested by some quartz that had newly fallen from the mountain. I dismounted and examined it; there was lots of it lying amongst more that had fallen a long time before and had become so weather-stained as not to attract the attention of a passer-by. I decided that Mount Stephen needed prospecting and planned to do that later on.

The horses, for which I had come, were not at the slough, so I followed the river to another feeding ground just below the site of the present town of Field. No animals were there. It was clear that they had been there and their tracks showed in which direction they had departed. I tracked them past the Natural Bridge where I noted that they had adopted the single file system, as though following a leader that knew where it was going. I became more convinced of this fact as the single file system continued without evidence of the horses having made any halts.

Through the bush, across small streams, then a little way up the mountain sides the tracks led me. After a time they returned to valley level alongside a creek that a few minutes later brought me to a beautiful sheet of water. I stood at the outlet of the mountain scenic gem known today as Emerald Lake.

The discovery of Emerald Lake is a telling example of the depth of knowledge of the country possessed by the Native peoples of the region. Native peoples knew the country intimately. Even their horses knew more about the coun-

Mt. Stephen towers above the Kicking Horse Valley. In its shadow lies the town of Field. The lower shoulder or "the nose" of Mt. Stephen is quite visible in this early photograph. It was below this "nose" that Tom Wilson discovered mineral traces that eventually led to the opening of the Monarch and Kicking Horse mines. (Photo courtesy of the Whyte Museum of the Canadian Rockies.)

try than the invading Europeans. Anyone who has worked with horses in the mountains will appreciate Wilson's analysis of how they were able to show him the way to Emerald Lake:

For a few moments I sat on my horse and enjoyed the rare, peaceful beauty of the scene, then, at the far end of the lake I noticed something move. It was an old white horse that belonged to my bunch and which we had bought from the Stoneys. I rode to the end of the lake and found the wanderers fairly revelling in one of the finest mountain meadows.

How had they found it? Well, I later figured that out.

Some years earlier, Cline, the Hudson's Bay factor at Jasper House, had arranged with the Kootenay and Shuswap Indians to meet him on the east side of the Great Divide to do their annual trading. This became necessary because of the enmity of the Blackfoot confederacy; the latter had practically forced the

45

British Columbia Indians to abandon trading at Jasper House by inflicting several defeats on them.

Cline had a special trail cut up the Maligne River to Maligne Lake, over Cataract Pass, then down what is known today as Cline River, to the big plains of the Saskatchewan. There he met the Kootenays and Shuswaps with his packtrain of trade goods and received from them their furs, etc. in exchange. That annual trade meeting gave the locality the name Kootenay Plains, a name that has often puzzled people when trying to discover its origin.

The Kootenays and Shuswaps had many enemies therefore, when setting out for their annual trade, they dared not leave their families and chattels to fall prey to those enemies. A whole tribe with its belongings travelled until well on the route, then encamped their families, old men and extra horses, in "hidden valleys" to await the braves' return from the Kootenay Plains. This system of trade ceased during the early '70's and was followed by the British Columbia Indians and the Stonies paying alternate annual visits to each other for the purposes of feasting, dancing and trading.

Some of the horses that we had purchased from the Stonies carried Kootenay or Shuswap brands; they proved that the Stonies had obtained the horses from their original owners at some of the annual festive-trading meets. It was evident that the pasture where I found them was one of the B.C. Indians' "hidden valleys" and the natural conclusion was that one, if not more of our horses had, when belonging to Shuswap or Kootenay, been left there for safety. While hunting food in the Kicking Horse sloughs, the horses had remembered the good feed in the "hidden valley" and with unerring instinct had led the rest of the bunch to there. That is the conclusion I arrived at and, right or wrong, it is certain that the incident resulted in the discovery of Emerald Lake.

Upon leaving the Kicking Horse Valley at the end of the season, Wilson picked up more samples of the "glittering rock" he had found below Mt. Stephen. The samples were later sent to J. J. McVicar in Salt Lake City. McVicar, the most famous assayer in the West at that time, reported that the samples were rich in lead, with zinc, antimony, and traces of silver, but that unless the ore was in large bodies near transportation to a smelter, it would require more money than Wilson had to mine it. Wilson decided to leave mining possibilities in Yoho unexplored for the time being. It would not be long, however, before others would see that potential and act on it.

Instead of returning to the south for the winter as was his custom, Wilson stayed in the Kananaskis area that winter not far from where Major Hurd had taken up residence. In the spring of 1883, Wilson returned to the summit of Kicking Horse Pass. The railway was advancing rapidly past Maple Creek in Saskatchewan and was expected to reach Calgary in the summer. By the end of the season, after further doubts about the superiority of Kicking Horse Pass over Howse Pass were finally resolved, the steel advanced as far as Silver City, below Castle Mountain. The next season the tracks would reach the Great Divide and cross Kicking Horse Pass into British Columbia.

Tom Wilson's surveying work with the railway came to an end. He became a prospector and later joined the Steele Scouts and fought in the Riel Rebellion. At the conclusion of his military service, Wilson returned to Morley to visit friends. While he was there a train arrived and a conductor who knew him asked if he was coming along on the ride to Craigellachie to watch the driving of the last spike. After the ceremony, Wilson shook hands and bade Major Rogers a fond farewell.

"Tom," the Major said, "One day we'll take a holiday and ride ocean to ocean on this railroad." But Wilson never saw Rogers again. While working with the Great Northern Railway in the Coeur d'Alene Mountains in Idaho in 1889, Rogers fell from a horse and, in May of that year, died from his injuries. Just as Rogers had predicted, Tom Wilson went on to live in the mountains for the rest of his life. In time, he became the most famous outfitter and guide in the Rockies, the man to see if you wanted access to the wilderness of the Great Divide.

FIELD HILL.

The Field Hill became the focal point for the railway engineer's courage on their trans-Canada trek.

Chapter 3

....

The Big Hill

The final decision to use Kicking Horse Pass as the rail route over the Great Divide of the Rockies has often been criticized because of the problems the steep grade and rugged terrain caused engineers and maintenance crews. A. B. Rogers came under fire even before the line over the pass was complete. Railway construction crews, working for construction companies contracted to build the line, complained that the line Rogers took down the pass entailed higher construction costs than necessary. But Rogers was under strict orders not to run any stretch of the rail grade over 2.5 percent. This limit on the slope of the grade demanded that the line be kept high on the mountainsides, where construction costs were high and work was difficult to complete. The construction companies, however, were allowed slopes of up to 4.5 percent so that they could keep to the lower mountainsides, where the construction was easier.

Leaving the top of the pass, Rogers's survey line kept to the maximum 2.5 percent through the heavy timber and the boulders described by Wilson as he descended into the valley in search of young Albert Rogers. The route sloped gently downhill over treacherous rock slides until it reached "the nose" on Mt. Stephen. This "nose" is a shoulderlike projection of the mountain that pushes far into the valley at its base, causing the Kicking Horse River to bend around it. It had been just beneath this nose that Tom Wilson and Fred Palling had found A. B. Rogers's starving nephew. Rogers's route had called for two very expensive tunnels through the nose about 150 metres above the valley floor. After passing Mt. Stephen, the proposed line was to continue down the valley at the 2.5 percent grade. After passing about 90 metres above the present location of Field, the route would gradually drop to the level of the top of the Ottertail Hill before following the Kicking Horse River slowly downhill toward its junction with the Beaverfoot. The route was designed to leave Yoho by following the Kicking Horse through its wild canyon to its confluence with the Columbia near Golden.

The construction company, however, did not follow Rogers's proposed route but chose a much steeper and more direct route down Kicking Horse Pass. In running the line steeply down into the valley, the company was able to avoid expensive tunnelling, heavy rock cutting, and the dangerous rock and gravel slides that posed problems on Rogers's route. After passing the nose on Mt. Stephen, the bed was side-cut into the rock until it reached water level in the bottom of the valley at the present site of Field. From Field westward the line rose up the Ottertail Hill in such a steep a grade that for years it could only be climbed by trains with pusher units attached to them.

Although the Rogers route would have been more expensive to build, it would have saved the railway a fortune in the long run. The 13 kilometres of grade on either side of Mt. Stephen as per the Rogers-Hurd plan would have cost from $100,000 to $125,000 in 1885 dollars to construct. This amount, however, is only a fraction of what it later cost to maintain the line up the "Big Hill" for the 23 years it took to deal with the impractical line the construction company followed. The cost of building the line using Rogers's route in the first place would have saved the railway millions in the long term. In 1908 the railway spent millions to carve spiral tunnels through Mt. Ogden in order to reduce the grade on the west side of Kicking Horse Pass. But these were difficult times and the cost of the railway was threatening to bankrupt the land. Were it not for these difficult times and the "Big Hill" on Kicking Horse Pass, there may never had been a town named Field.

Overcoming Obstacles

By the fall of 1883, the tracks had been laid from the east as far as the approach to Kicking Horse Pass. From the west the tracks had been advanced as far as the western slopes of the Gold Range. Less than 300 kilometres of railroad remained to be built between the two advancing lines of Canada's national railway. That relatively short section would take two years to build. There were a number of serious obstacles. On the western side of the Selkirks there was Notch Hill, Eagle Pass, and finally the spine of the Selkirks at Rogers Pass. Along the Great Divide was the difficult passage down the west side of Kicking Horse Pass, as well as the gorge of Kicking Horse Canyon farther west.

Work on the railway was slow to begin in that wet spring of 1884. Deep snow lingered long into the spring, making work difficult and dangerous. By May 25, the tracks at last crested the divide, a cause for some celebration. The steep descent down the pass delayed further progress until July. After tote roads were built, the grading slowly continued in advance of the laying of the track. Deciding that the originally surveyed route would take years to build, the contracting company proposed constructing a "temporary" line that would descend from the summit of the pass to the valley floor at twice the slope proposed by Rogers and Hurd. Critics of the plan argued that such a slope would make the Kicking Horse Pass section of the Canadian Pacific Railway the steepest main line in the Western Hemisphere.

Undaunted as ever, William Cornelius Van Horne arrived on the scene to

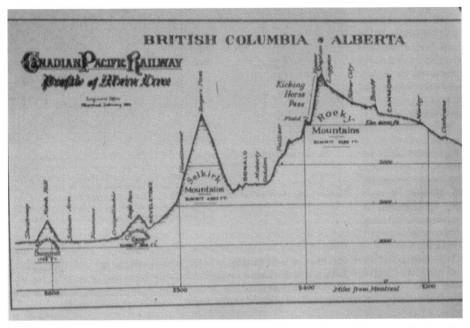

The significance of Kicking Horse Pass as an obstacle to the building of the Canadian Pacific Railway can be seen clearly in the profile the tracks take across the mountains of Alberta and British Columbia. (Photograph courtesy of Canadian Pacific Photographic Services.)

survey the problem. After much analysis, Van Horne argued that the cost of maintaining special locomotives for a short, steep push up the pass made for less expense and delay than a slow, more gradual climb up a lesser grade. In a flourish of modern logic, Van Horne's argument pivoted around the idea that the construction of a temporary line could permit the Canadian Pacific a number of years in which to observe weather patterns, stream flows, glacial activity, and the frequency of avalanches before a final decision about the route needed to be made. The fact of the matter was that the railway could afford to do little else. The Big Hill was part of the political cost of moving the main line 300 kilometres south from Yellowhead Pass to be closer to the American border. At this crucial stage in the railway's construction, the cost of reducing the grade at the Great Divide was beyond the means of the railway because it was beyond the means of the nation.

The entire Big Hill project was labour intensive. The line required continuous maintenance, as did the pusher trains and the standard locomotives that pulled the regular service trains. It was clear that a railway service centre was going to be necessary to keep the Big Hill open even in summer. A small yard and engine facility was laid out on the valley floor at the foot of Mt. Stephen, and a stone roundhouse was constructed to service the locomotives. For a num-

Pusher units like these were used to ensure that trains made it safely up the Big Hill. These units were used less and less after the Spiral Tunnel was completed and as locomotives and track technology improved. (Photo courtesy of Canadian Pacific Archives.)

ber of months this burgeoning community was simply called Third Siding. In December 1884, Donald Smith, the railway syndicate's great financier, came to the end of the tracks. A few months earlier he had encouraged Cyrus West Field, a wealthy Chicago businessman and the promoter of the first Atlantic communications cable, to come and see the potential of the railway for himself. In an attempt to pursuade Field to invest in the financially troubled railway, Smith, with a sweep of his hand, named the little railway community and the mountain across the valley from it in Field's honour. Despite the honor, Field, did not commit any money to the venture. The little town grew anyway. Even before the construction of its grand hotel, it was famous for its proximity to the increasingly notorious Big Hill.

Since the Trans-Canada Highway follows the original 4.5 percent grade down the Big Hill into the valley of the Kicking Horse, a grade of this slope no longer seems very imposing. In 1884, however, a 4.5 percent grade was a serious matter. It meant that the front end of a locomotive of a five-car passenger train would be about 5 metres higher in altitude than the rear of the last passenger car when it went up the Big Hill. Steam locomotives going up such hills had to be full of water to prevent their boilers from exploding, and even a passenger train of only a few cars would need pusher engines to help it up the Big Hill. Such a steep grade also pushed contemporary brake technology to its very limits. To prevent runaways on the Big Hill, three runaway tracks were built. Switches on special sidings faced trains that were headed downhill, ready to turn the sidings into runaway lanes that climbed upward at an opposite angle to the main line so that runaway trains would quickly lose momentum. The switches leading to the runaway lanes were always open. Every train had to come to a complete stop upgrade of each switch before it would be turned to allow the train to continue downhill. As early Big Hill railroader Roxy Hamilton commented, there was a big difference of opinion as to how well this system worked. He argued that the first siding saved some trains because at that point on the descent the downward speed was not great enough to make the siding impossible to take: "As for the other two, about all you did was to pile up a train in the siding instead of down the mountain."

At the time the railway was completed, the Rockies and the Selkirks generally received much more snow than generally falls today. Rotary plows like this one were used everywhere in the Rockies. (Photograph courtesy of Canadian Pacific Archives.)

Judge Matthew Begbie, the Chief Justice of British Columbia, described an early journey he made down the Big Hill on his way to Revelstoke. This account was published in an article entitled The Big Hill by Edward E. Pugsley, Railroad Magazine, September, 1946. He particularly remembered the three famous switchbacks:

You come down dead slow — about 4 mls. per hr., with 2 engines, one ahead and one astern, lest the train shd. take charge and run down hill by the force of gravity. As a further protection against this, and what has a wonder-

fully footling effect upon nervous people, I shd. think, there have been provided at the more dangerous, i.e.: precipitous places, short deviations, about 200 to 300 … yards long, running uphill — and into which the pointsmen, if they see you running away, and if they are near enough to the points, can turn you, if not at one place, at least at another or a third.

The good judge was describing what could be a perilous descent of nearly 400 metres from the pass to the valley floor. If a train got out of control, it might be able to be switched to one of the runaway tracks — if it wasn't moving too fast. If a train built up too much speed, it would be unable to make some of the tight turns on the track to reach the safety switches. Even if it reached a runaway lane, it could still thunder into oblivion off the steep incline of the track. A train is not like a car when it leaves the road; derailment is an awesome and often fatal event.

As safety devices, the runaway sidings on the Big Hill were of little benefit to a long train, of, say, 16 cars, running completely out of control for 20 kilometres into the valley. Political and construction considerations aside, the entire Big Hill project seemed idiotic right from the start. Money and time were saved, but at the expense of overall safety. There were some terrible wrecks. Early in

Early bridges were not always made of steel. In the western mountains extensive use of timber was common in the construction of some of the largest and highest bridges on the entire rail line. This huge wooden span crossed the Ottertail River. (Photograph courtesy of Canadian Pacific Archives.)

Early visitors were enthraled by the Continental Divide and most of the passenger trains stopped there. The waters of Divide Creek split here, some going east into the Atlantic and the rest flowing west into the Pacific. Divide Creek is not natural. Railway superintendent John Niblock divided the creek into two with a shovel.

1884, construction train 146 steamed out of Hector near the top of Kicking Horse Pass pulling flatcars loaded with heavy bridge timbers. One hundred and twenty men were on board. Suddenly the train began to pick up speed. With brakeshoes screaming, the train began to thunder down the grade. Men started jumping for their lives. The train reached nearly 130 kilometres an hour before it telescoped into a mountainside, where the huge timbers splintered like match sticks. Hissing with escaping steam, the engine then plunged into the frothing waters of the Kicking Horse far below. Sixty men had to be treated in the railway's hospital car. In another incident, the engineer of work train 145 also lost control. Halfway down the second 4.4 percent switch, the train began to quickly gather speed. Just ahead was a tunnel in which 60 men were working. The engineer slammed the brakes into reverse, set the whistle, and jumped. Luckily the tender derailed, and miraculously, the drawbar held, stopping the train.

It took only a wreck or two for the Big Hill to develop a Big Reputation. Heavier engines with bigger and more efficient air brakes were brought out west to replace lighter locomotives with inadequate hand brake systems. Double-braked cars were also brought out just for this section. If they were heavily loaded, waiting trains were sometimes chained to the tracks to prevent runaways. Prime Minister John A. Macdonald came out west on the second train to have crossed the country. His amazingly daring wife, Agnes, rode on the cowcatcher through Kicking Horse Canyon to prove how safe the line was.

It was a highly successful public relations stunt that did nothing to ameliorate the hazard of the Big Hill.

It is a great credit to the men who worked on that section that there were not more accidents. To have worked on the Big Hill was the railway equivalent of the big leagues. Only the very best engineers and brakemen worked the trains up and down the pass. While the railway continued to study the conditions of the route through Kicking Horse Pass, the line was kept open with remarkably few incidents for nearly 15 years. When a 10-car coal train tore out of control and jumped the track, its engineer, Jack Ladner of Revelstoke, and a young fireman named Aimslee died in the wreck. The railway knew then that it was time to reconsider how the trains got up and down Kicking Horse Pass. Spiral tunnels near the pass were proposed. By this time the town of Field was a thriving railway service centre and hopping tourist resort.

The Dominion's Great Surveyors

A rash of mountain naming had gone on around Field after the last spike was driven. In 1886, Mt. Stephen was named after George Stephen, the president of the Bank of Montreal and one-time president of the Canadian Pacific Railway. Another giant that towers over the little town of Field is Mt. Burgess. It was also named in 1886, by surveyor Otto Klotz for Alexander MacKinnon Burgess, one-time Deputy Minister of the Interior who became Canada's Commissioner of Public Lands in 1897. In 1916, another mountain overlooking Field was named for Lieutenant Colonel John Stoughton Dennis, who, for a time, was the Surveyor General of Canada. Despite all the important-sounding names of the mountains around it, Field was just a little town in the bottom of a canyonlike valley in the middle of a beautiful but dangerous nowhere.

Even with railway completed, much of the mountain West was still remote, save for the narrow strip of country flanking the rail line. Before the potential for the resources and tourism in the West could truly be appreciated, the region had to be mapped. Starting at the fringes of the railway belt, a small army of highly dedicated surveyors began to establish a picture of what the mountains were like north and south of the line. Although mountains and lakes have been named for some of these unsung heroes, most of their efforts have been forgotten today.

By the terms of Confederation, a corridor 32 kilometres on either side of the rail right-of-way was to be conveyed by British Columbia to the federal government as part of British Columbia's payment for its share in the cost of the railway. In order to clearly define which of the mountains lay within the 64 kilometre-wide belt adjoining the tracks, a comprehensive survey was demanded. This was to be a real survey, describing the timber, minerals, and agricultural features of the landscape right to the tops of the mountains. The model for the system was to be the system of rectangular townships that had already been

Though very expensive, the Spiral Tunnels reduced the grade on the Big Hill to what Rogers had originally proposed. (Photograph courtesy of Canadian Pacific Archives.)

adopted by earlier surveys of the prairies. Clearly this was going to be a difficult task in such a jumbled landscape. The railway, running right through the centre of the grid, became the platform from which the survey was to be conducted.

The preliminary work for the great survey was straightforward even by Victorian standards. The year after the railway was completed, Otto Klotz, assistant astronomer to the Department of the Interior, made a compass declination survey from the height of the Rockies at Kicking Horse Pass to a position near Revelstoke where his survey overlapped a similar survey conducted by William Ogilvie, who had worked eastward from the coast. In the course of these surveys, Klotz also established the position and altitude of the major peaks of the Selkirks adjacent to the railway. Reference marks for each of these surveys were located at every mile on the rail route, and these became points of reference for additional, more detailed work.

A very astute and highly motivated individual happened to be the Surveyor General of Dominion Lands at the time. Édouard Deville realized that three-month summer field seasons in the high mountains were too short to keep the survey ahead of development spurred by the railway. The ability to cover a large area in a short time became crucial to the success of his surveying project. Deville, who had been born and trained in France, knew that the emerging science of photography had already been applied to surveying as early as 1849. He predicted that this new technology might help to make better

Much was made of the engineering that was required to complete the Spiral Tunnels. Photographs were made to demonstrate how the tunnels worked. As early trains were not long enough to curl around the entire length of the tunnels, double exposures were made showing where the train went in and where it came out of each of the two "corkscrews." Trains today are now long enough to demonstrate how the tunnels work without resorting to trick photography. (Photograph courtesy of Canadian Pacific Archives.)

use of the short field season, while allowing follow-up work to be done between seasons in a warm, comfortable office. The process, developed by one of Deville's mentors, had already been successfully used in Germany, Austria, Italy, Switzerland, and the United States. The new system had obvious advantages over the traditional method of plane-table surveying used in Canada. The photographic method required that fewer measurements be taken and that key references on photographic plates be plotted for off-season study.

There were only two serious drawbacks to the new technology. First, the photographs had to be of the highest quality, taken under the clearest atmospheric conditions. This would be a problem in the West, since steam locomotives often spewed live coals from their smokestacks, causing heavy smoke and forest fires along the rail line. The second drawback was that the photographs had to be taken from high positions, and in the Rockies this meant the summits of mountains. The mountains did not have to be the highest in any given area, or the most difficult to climb. But mountains had to be climbed. A first generation of homegrown mountaineers was instantly created by the demands of this new surveying technology.

One of the narrow gauge locomotives used to excavate the Spiral Tunnels lies on its side near Kicking Horse campground. There is some debate whether this locomotive was wrecked or if it was simply cannibalized to repair other locomotives used in the project.

Kicking Horse Pass still poses a considerable railway maintenance problem. In September of 1978, a combined rock and mud slide came down from the shoulders of Cathedral Mountain and nearly buried this locomotive.

The First Ascent of Mt. Stephen

One of the most active of the government surveyors in the Rockies and the Selkirk Mountains was James Joseph McArthur, who worked on the survey between 1886 and 1892. During this period, McArthur surveyed the rail line all the way from Canmore, on the eastern edge of the Rockies, to the summit of the Gold Range west of Revelstoke. On September 9, 1887, J. J. McArthur, accompanied by his assistant, T. Riley, climbed Mt. Stephen from the town of Field. They did so with little previous experience and under the encumbrance of heavy sur-

59

veying equipment and cameras. McArthur and Riley deserve to be remembered for their incredible feat. The climb must have been an epic, in fact, for the usually stolid McArthur was not one to exaggerate difficulties. The ascent of 3199 metre Mt. Stephen is no easy walk. Here is what McArthur wrote about the climb in the government blue book in which he was instructed by the department to keep his surveying notes:

Started at 4:30 on September 9, 1887. The slope leading to the top of the blade-like ridge was very steep and covered with slaty debris, which carried us back at every step. Any attempt to sit down resulted in being carried with an avalanche of shale a considerable distance before we could arrest ourselves. Viewing the sharp, broken declivities up which we would have to climb before we should reach the turret-shaped cliffs at the top, we began to realise the dangers and difficulties of the task. Perpendicular walls often rose before us, the only possible way up which lay through sharp V-shaped gorges broken by short precipices. We had to keep close together and exercise great care, as the displacing of one stone caused a perfect avalanche of rock and gravel. Reaching the base of the turret, we started up another gorge. Progress at times was not much greater than on a treadmill, as the sliding gravel set in motion by our feet poured with continuous roar over the precipices below. At last a perpendicular wall, several hundred feet high, rose before us.

Foot by foot we made our way, cutting steps as we ascended, and in time reached the ledge of the rock and looked down the perilous slope. A slip on the glare surface meant death, and how we were going to get down again caused no little anxiety. Crawling along dangerous ledges and up steep narrow gorges, we groped our way. At length we reached the top of what we had judged from below to be the highest point on the mountain. But another wall arose several hundred feet higher. We moved along to a slanting rift, up which we clambered, sometimes dependent for a hold on the first joints of our fingers. After a perilous climb of about a hundred feet we arrived at a debris-covered slope leading to the top of the ridge. It was like a much-broken wall, in some places not more than three feet wide. It required all our nerve to crawl about the eighth of a mile on the top of one of these half-balanced masses to the highest point on the mountain, 6,385 feet above the railway track.

Further surveys were often required if the photographic conditions were not quite right. McArthur climbed the mountain a second time, on August 31, 1892. On this ascent, he and his fellow climbers carried a flag and a 4 metre pole upon which the flag would be flown.

It is difficult to imagine the hardships these men endured. J. J. McArthur and his peers were unassuming men, truly Victorian in their understatement of difficulty and danger. Using the railway as a centre for their operations, they set off to discover new valleys, passes, and mountains. Just like Hector and Rogers before them, they were often without provisions. Although they knew their bearings, they were often lost in totally alien valleys, many of which had not even been visited by Native peoples. They were constantly encountering bears. The smoke of summer forest fires, often sparked by locomotives, fouled their work. Only very exceptional men could qualify for such travail. Describing McArthur's work, Arthur Wheeler, a famous surveyor in his own right, had this to say about McArthur the man:

$\mathcal{H}$*e is a quiet, unassuming man, who has probably climbed more mountains in these regions than any other person, and has made a large number of firstascents. No flourish of trumpets ushered him forth to conquest, no crown of laurels awaited his victory; a corps of trained Swiss guides was not at hand to place his footsteps, to check his down-slidings and select for him the surest road. With one assistant, transit and camera on back, many a perilous climb has been made, the rope only being used in the case of the most urgent need. In all kinds of weather; through snow, over ice and in pouring rain, many a difficult ascent has been accomplished, many privations encountered and much hardship endured; the only record being a few terse paragraphs in a Department Bluebook — short as they are, they are worth reading.*

James Joseph McArthur is one of Canada's unsung heroes. McArthur made important contributions to the first complete maps of the Rockies and was also one of the country's first competent native born mountaineers. (Photograph courtesy of the Department of Mines and Resources, Canada.)

McArthur did more climbing, and climbed at a very much higher standard, than many later climbers who gained fame from their holiday experiences in the Rockies. It is fitting that Lake McArthur in Yoho National Park was named for this great surveyor.

The railway bridge over the Kicking Horse River at the top of the Field Hill can still be seen today beside the Trans-Canada highway.

Chapter 4

The Birth of Tourism in Yoho

The national dream was completed in November 1885. Unfortunately, projected freight and domestic passenger traffic was not of sufficient volume to subsidize the winter upkeep of the line through the formidable mountains of the West. As the most expensive public project ever undertaken in this country, the newly completed railway was going to have to find creative ways to pay for itself. William Cornelius Van Horne had already been thinking about the opportunities the stunning scenery of the West might present to foreign visitors. Thus, for the first time, North America's spectacular landscapes were seen to have an economic value.

An astute executive, Van Horne believed that the burgeoning aesthetic of the Romantics, as expressed by writers and poets such as Goethe, Shelley, Wordsworth, and Blake, could be used to fuel the engines of the railway's great westbound trains. According to the Romantic view, Nature mirrored the soul's journey toward perfection and mountains embodied the shape of the spiritual climb. Almost overnight the land of the West, with its stupendous peaks and roaring rivers, became a symbol of the bounty of this young country. Thus, the idea of tourism in Canada was born. The image of the aesthetic ideal was made concrete in extensive promotion in Europe and in the eastern United States. Canada became the natural wonder of the Western world. The changing aesthetic of the Romantics had charged wild landscapes with a new spiritual energy, and wealthy travellers were prepared to pay handsomely for the opportunity to look upon unspoiled nature.

Even before the rails were laid through the Rockies, tourism for the wealthy had helped pay for other sections of the line. This gave impetus to what was hoped would be a very lucrative tourism business in the West. Nowhere along the main line of the CPR was the country more spectacular than in British Columbia. It was with good reason that the railway had especially big plans for the mountain sections of the line. Van Horne envisioned a chain of grand railway hotels stretching over the entire West. The chalets and rustic tourist cabins that would be built would rival anything of their kind in the world. But Van Horne was interested in more than just buildings. A man who was ahead of his time, Van Horne saw that the raw, wild nature of the country was an attraction that mountain destinations in Europe had already begun to lose. Van Horne believed, as many people did at the time, that private business interests in areas of natural beauty often compromised the very qualities visitors might have come to see.

Citing Niagara Falls as a gross example of what could go wrong with tourism, a movement was afoot in the early 1880s to establish special legal status for at least some of the natural wonders of the West. Using Yellowstone in the United States as an example, Van Horne and others argued successfully for the creation of a number of public reserves to be protected against excessive commercial development. The first of these was the Banff Hot Springs Reserve, a 26-square kilometre (10-square-mile) park created in 1885 to protect the natural hot springs that bubbled out from the base of Sulphur Mountain near Banff. Yoho, Canada's second national park, was created by an Order-In-Council on October 10, 1886. All 26 square kilometres (10 square miles) of it were set aside around Mt. Stephen in the Kicking Horse Valley and included the Big Hill section of the railway. Glacier National Park, at the summit of Rogers Pass, was set aside at the same time. Later expanded into much larger reserves, these three fledgling parks received the full support of the Canadian Pacific Railway, which immediately set to building grand hotels close to the parks.

The Grand Hotels

The first grand hotel was planned for Banff. With the hot springs as a natural attraction, a big hotel was planned on a site overlooking the Bow Valley near the springs. Smaller railway hotels were planned at convenient intervals at Field, Rogers Pass, and North Bend. A chalet was also built later at Lake Louise. Mt. Stephen House in Field and Glacier House near the summit of Rogers Pass would serve the railway in other ways besides tourism. The Big Hill and other grades like it presented more than just technical problems for the CPR. Not only were the grades steep, treacherous, and in need of continuous maintenance, it was also very difficult and rather dangerous to push and pull heavy dining cars over them. At Kicking Horse Pass and Rogers Pass, where the trains faced the steepest grades, hotels were built to offer meal services for passengers travelling between the Rockies and the Pacific coast. Although they have not survived, these two hotels were grand places to visit in their time.

Construction of Mt. Stephen House began in the spring of 1886 on a site on the north side of the tracks, a hundred metres or so east of Field station. Designed by railway architect Thomas Sorby, with much advice from a very interested and involved William Van Horne, it was a very small structure composed mostly of dining space, with a few rooms for overnight guests. Since service on the main line had already begun, dining cars were parked on a siding at Field to serve train passengers. Mt. Stephen House opened in the autumn of

Twin Falls in the Yoho Valley, CAROLE HARMON

Lake Lefroy and Mt. Hungabee near Lake O'Hara, STEPHEN HUTCHINGS

The Wiwaxy Peaks from the Opabin Plateau, STEPHEN HUTCHINGS

Lake O'Hara, R.W. SANDFORD

Takakkaw Falls and the Yoho Valley, CAROLE HARMON

The Goodsirs, STEPHEN HUTCHINGS

Takakkaw Falls, CAROLE HARMON

Emerald Lake and The President Mtn., CAROLE HARMON

Looking across Emerald Lake towards Mt. Carnarvon, CAROLE HARMON

Mt. Stephen and the Natural Bridge on the Kicking Horse River, STEPHEN HUTCHINGS

The Des Poilus Glacier with Mt. Des Poilus in the background, STEPHEN HUTCHINGS

Amiskwi Peak in winter, STEPHEN HUTCHINGS

This early photograph of Mt. Stephen House illustrates the great hotel after its expansion in 1902. The photograph also illustrates just how much of the valley forests had been burned over by the turn of the nineteenth century. Coal and wood burning steam trains caused extensive forest fires throughout the Rockies over more than two decades. (Photograph courtesy of Canadian Pacific Archives.)

1886. Glacier House and Fraser Canyon House at North Bend did not open until the following spring.

Although Banff and Lake Louise had higher profiles, it did not take rail passengers long to appreciate the stunning scenery that surrounded Mt. Stephen House. Field was close to the Natural Bridge on the Kicking Horse and Emerald Lake, where the CPR built a chalet in 1902. Waterfalls have always been a central attraction for visitors to Yoho. Only slightly lower than Della Falls on Vancouver Island, 380 metre Takakkaw Falls in the Yoho Valley was the second highest waterfall in Canada. Easily reached by saddle horse from Field, it became one of Yoho's earliest and most-visited attractions, and the railway built Yoho Valley Lodge near the falls. A small chalet was also built beneath Twin Falls at the head of the Yoho Valley. Word gradually went out that Yoho was worth a stop on the transcontinental route. In 1901, Mt. Stephen Park was expanded to 2145.6 square kilometres (828.5 square miles) and its name was changed to Yoho National Park. In 1902, architect Francis Rattenbury designed a massive expansion to the hotel. Mt. Stephen House became a luxurious and elegant entranceway to the glorious scenery of the Rockies. Located between Banff National Park and its famous hot springs and the dramatic scenery of Rogers Pass, Yoho was in the very centre of what the railway promoted as the Canadian Alps. The Canadian Pacific compressed all the ranges of mountains in the west into "Fifty Switzerlands in One; a mountain playground for the

Emerald Lake Lodge was just one of a number of railway-owned backcountry lodges in the Rockies. It was opened in the summer of 1902. (Photograph courtesy of Emerald Lake Lodge.)

world." Advertising slogans of this kind were not wasted on British and European adventurers, who saw in mountaineering the pursuit of the noblest of human ideals. Mt. Stephen House would soon become one of the earliest centres of alpinism in Canada's mountain West.

The Birth of Tourist Mountaineering

Mountaineering had formally evolved in Europe in the middle of the 18th century. The vanguard of the Romantic Movement sought mountains as places of purity and spiritual release. The Victorians expanded on the Romantic aesthetic by adding geographic exploration and scientific study to the ambitions of the mountaineer. The popularity of climbing received a great boost in the summer of 1865 when, after seven attempts, a British climber named Edward Whymper made the first ascent of the Matterhorn. This ascent might not have been noteworthy but for the fact that on the descent four of Whymper's party fell to their deaths on the glacier below. The accident caused a furor. There was talk of banning mountaineering. But the threat of banning mountaineering only made it more popular. Only 10 years after the accident on the Matterhorn, every major mountain in Europe had been climbed. European and British mountaineers had to look elsewhere for new summits to climb. It so happened that the completion of the Canadian Pacific Railway in 1885 coincided nicely with a growing European hunger for unknown, unnamed, and unclimbed peaks.

The first tourism explorer to come to Yoho was mathematician Jean Habel, who came from Berlin in the summer of 1897. Habel undertook a 17-day solitary expedition to the Yoho Valley by way of Emerald Lake and Yoho Pass. Habel travelled to the end of the Yoho Valley to the Wapta Icefield and returned along the Yoho Valley past Twin Falls and Takakkaw Falls, emerging at the junction of the Yoho River and the Kicking Horse River, about 6 kilometres from Field. Although Tom Wilson argued that he was the first to visit the Yoho in 1894, it is possible that Habel was the first to make a thorough exploration of the valley. On hearing Habel's account of the spectacular falls in the Yoho, the railway built a trail as far as Takakkaw in 1900. That same year, while Norman

Collie was climbing Mt. Balfour from the Banff side of the mountain, he named a big peak in the Yoho Valley Mt. Habel in honour of the German explorer and mountaineer. Politics intervened during World War I, however, and the name of Mt. Habel was changed to Mt. des Poilus, since it was considered inappropriate to name a beautiful Canadian mountain after a German. Des Poilus instead honors the lowly privates of the French army, a million and a half of whom died in that Great War. Although a stream that runs near Mt. Alberta in the Columbia Icefield area still bears his name, Jean Habel is practically forgotten today.

The first climbers in the Canadian West were also from overseas. They began to come as soon as the railway was in operation. Experienced mountaineers like William Spotswood Green, Carl Sulzer, and Emil Huber arrived in the Canadian Alps early enough to develop maps of the places they visited before they could be visited by Canadian surveyors. Wealthy Americans, who were usually introduced to climbing through visits to the Alps, also began coming to the Rockies and the Selkirks to make names for themselves. A golden age of mountaineering began quietly at Rogers Pass and in the Lake Louise area of the Rockies. Visitors simply stepped off the train and made their way from the tracks to the summits of unclimbed and usually unnamed peaks. Unfortunately, many of these climbers were novices. Some would get off the train with guidebooks in their hands telling them how to tie knots and use the ice axes they clumsily held in their hands. Without adequate training or experience, it was just a matter of time before accidents started to happen.

All hell broke loose in Canadian mountaineering on August 3, 1896. A party of Americans had left early in the morning from the log cabin chalet on the north shore of Lake Louise. Foremost among them was Charles Fay, president of the Appalachian Mountain Club and, later, founding president of the American Alpine Club. After crossing the lower Victoria Glacier, the party made its way up what is now known as the "Death Trap" to the summit of a

In 1901, James Hector (seated) made his way to Canada for the last time and was met in Revelstoke by the "Lion of the Matterhorn", Edward Whymper. (Whymper is standing.) Whymper was in Canada as a guest of the Canadian Pacific Railway. (Photograph courtesy of the Whyte Museum of the Canadian Rockies.)

75

high col between Mt. Victoria and Mt. Lefroy. The highest mountain yet to be surveyed in the Rockies to that date, Mt. Lefroy was their goal. Looking down into Yoho National Park, they continued to the highest shoulder of Mt. Lefroy. A hundred metres from the summit, one of the climbers, Phillip Stanley Abbot, unroped and advanced ahead of the others to forge a route past the last difficulties between the climbers and the summit. A moment later he hurtled past his companions to his death on the rocks below. Abbot's death caused much the same furor in North America as the death of Whymper's companions had caused in Europe. Mountaineering suddenly had almost as much of a profile in North America as it had in Europe. To avoid further accidents and the accompanying bad press, the CPR brought Swiss guides to Canada as part of the attraction of visiting the Canadian Alps. The appearance of the guides proved good for business, so much so that the railway sponsored a promotional visit by the conqueror of the Matterhorn. In the summer of 1901, Edward Whymper himself came to stay at Mt. Stephen House.

At 62 years of age, Whymper was finished with serious mountaineering. Moreover, years of drinking, which he attributed to the death of his companions on the Matterhorn, had reduced his vitality. Sponsored by the CPR, Whymper was supposedly in Canada to write travel articles to attract British and European adventurers to the Rockies. The railway had also hoped that Whymper would make international news by climbing his second Matterhorn, the "Matterhorn of the Rockies" — Mt. Assiniboine. Although Whymer did not ever climb Mt. Assiniboine, he did mightily influence a British mountaineer — James Outram — who climbed Mt. Assiniboine on Whymper's behalf.

The Mad Parson from Ipswich

James Outram first came to the Canadian Rockies in the summer of 1900. As vicar of St. Peter's in Ipswich, England, Outram (pronounced ooht-ram) had apparently overworked himself and suffered a nervous breakdown. It was this collapse that "impelled him to the mountain heights for mental rest and physical recuperation." Like Whymper, he made Field the centre of his Rocky Mountain activities, which included exploration of much of Yoho Park. From the moment he set eyes on Field, Outram knew it was the place for him. Outram's book In The Heart of the Canadian Rockies, published by Macmillan, London in 1905, is one of the first mountaineering classics to be written about Canada. In this book Outram has much to say about Yoho and especially about Field. It appears that Miss Jean Mollison ran a hospitable hotel:

My happiest recollections of the Rockies centre round Field. The pleasant sojourn of a week in 1900 led to its becoming my headquarters for the next two years. The little Chalet of the former seasons and the larger Hotel that now exists were alike pervaded with a home-like atmosphere due to the personality of

Miss Mollison, who "made" Field as an abiding-place.

Nestling close under the gigantic precipices of Mt. Stephen, beset on either side by rugged mountain-crags, the little hamlet stands beside the eddying, glacial waters of the Kicking Horse River. Far up, the valley narrows to the Pass of the Divide; far down, the mighty pyramids of the Van Horne Range, their ruddy slopes streaked with snow and usually softened with deep purple shadows or wreathed in billowy clouds, complete the circle of majestic heights.

The only thing that bothered Outram about this mountain paradise was the extent of damage done by forest fires. Early photographs of the valley illustrate what Outram was talking about. After the railway went through, there was hardly a tree left to be found anywhere in any of the lower valleys. Outram and his brother, William, walked from Laggan Station at the top of the divide near Lake Louise to Field. It sickened him to see how much of the park had been burned:

The curse of fire, alas, has devastated thousands of acres of the grand primeval forests of the Rockies....Civilization has its drawbacks as well as its advantages. The careless trapper or prospector, the construction gang of railroad enterprise, have all contributed to the great change from Nature's untouched glory to these too frequent scenes of desolation.

These fires are one of the saddest features of the mountain districts. The ravages of the past are visible in almost every valley; and every year fresh areas of living green are being swept by the pitiless flames and left a melancholy wilderness. The ease with which a forest fire is started is astounding and only rivalled by the rapidity of its progress when once it gains a hold upon the trees, and by the extent of the destruction ere the blaze is quenched. A single lighted match thrown carelessly upon the ground, a shower of sparks from a passing locomotive, a camp-fire insufficiently extinguished, may be the origin. And from this tiny cause, "how great a matter a little fire kindleth."

In September of 1900, Outram climbed Mt. Stephen with his brother and Swiss guide Christian Hasler. From the summit Outram could see Mt. Assiniboine to the south and the three-headed mass of Mt. Goodsir to the west. Marvelling at the boldness of McArthur's first two ascents, Outram descended to Field, stopping to fill his rucksack with fossils he found in huge numbers in the shales. After a failed attempt to make a first ascent of the main peak of Cathedral Mountain, James Outram returned home vowing to return the following season. On August 26, a year later, Outram returned to complete the ascent of Cathedral Mountain. By this time he had already met Edward Whymper, and it was Whymper who lent him the assistance of two Swiss guides for the climb. With Christian Klucker and Joseph Bossonney on the rope, Outram was able to make an elegant first ascent of the steep Cathedral wall.

The fortuitous meeting between James Outram and the great mountaineer Edward Whymper occurred as a result of a dispute between the aging and rather arrogant mountaineer and his outfitter. Whymper had arrived in the Rockies in June of 1901. His first investigations of the backcountry had begun on June 18 when Whymper, his four Swiss guides, and a photographer named W. G. Francklyn followed James Hector's route up Vermilion Pass and down into what is now Kootenay National Park. The outfitter was Bill Peyto, one of the area's best and most famous horsemen and guides. After climbing a number of smaller mountains, including the mountain that now bears Whymper's name, the expedition returned to Banff. Whymper moved operations to the Lake Louise area and then to the Yoho Valley, where the bulk of 1901 first ascents would be made. It is here that relations between Whymper and the rest of the party began to deteriorate.

According to the story later told by Peyto, Whymper maintained such an air of superiority about him that he offended everyone around him. Especially put out were his four guides, Christian Klucker, James Pollinger, Joseph Bossonney, and Hans Kaufmann, who felt that Whymper was treating them as porters instead of the qualified guides they were. Peyto, who believed that everybody was pretty much equal in the backcountry, was not exactly shy about expressing his feelings toward Whymper. He was, quite simply, not going to be made to feel inferior by anybody. After moving Whymper's camp from Yoho Pass to the upper Yoho Valley, Peyto returned to Banff on the grounds that the horses were sick, leaving Whymper without logistical support. An enraged Whymper thundered down to Field to find a new outfitter. In Field, Whymper ran into Tom Wilson, who offered Tom Martin as replacement for Peyto. Wilson also introduced Whymper to the man who would do for the Rockies what Whymper did for the Alps — the Reverend James Outram. Perhaps because they were of similar social standing, Whymper invited Outram to join his camp. Outram recorded how the journey began.

On August 6th, 1901, Mr Whymper and I, with Christian Klucker (one of Mr. Whymper's four Swiss guides), Christian Hasler and Tom Martin, spent a day in following up the North Branch of the Kicking Horse [now the Amiskwi River] to the mouth of its chief tributary, Kiwetinok Creek. This stream rises near Kiwetinok Pass, which separates its head-waters from those of the Upper Yoho Valley, where Mr. Whymper's camp was situated, and our object was to reconnoitre this side in order to find out whether a satisfactory route could be made from the camp to Field by way of the intervening pass.

James Outram spent two weeks with Whymper in the Yoho Valley, during which several new mountains were climbed. Four first ascents were made, including Mt. Habel, Mt. Collie, Trolltinder Mountain, and Isolated Peak. During this time, perhaps as a way of relieving hard feelings in his entourage,

Mt. Pollinger was named for Whymper's Swiss guide James Pollinger and Michael Peak for Arthur Michael, a prominent member of the Appalachian Mountain Club and one of Whymper's most respected friends. Although the climbs the party made in the Yoho Valley were interesting, they were not, at least in technical terms, difficult. This expedition was noteworthy mainly for its unusual observations of the wildlife and natural features of the Yoho Valley. In the following passage Outram describes the discovery of a porcupine on the Habel Glacier. Perhaps it is human arrogance that makes us surprised to find animals migrating across the ice, but we are not the only mountaineers. Although not seen regularly, animals have been spotted on glaciers in the Rocky Mountains for a long time.

A*t 11:30 we left the top to return to camp by way of Isolated Peak and the eastern glacier. As we skirted the ice-cliffs above the Habel Glacier, we espied upon the snow, close to the edge of a wide-yawning crevasse, a dark, round object, which at first we could not recognize. Changing our course to get a nearer view, we saw it was a monster porcupine. But whether he was dead, asleep, or wrapped in meditation, it was impossible to tell. Venturing as far as was prudent to the upper lip of the crevasse which separated us, I photographed this candidate for alpine honours, and then, to find out his condition, ignobly snow-balled him. This took immediate effect. At the indignity, he hastily uncurled himself and waddled off along the rim of the deep fissure. Again I took his portrait, just before he disappeared behind an icy projection. A moment later we saw him try to turn, but, alas, he slipped and fell, and the last seen of the unhappy mountaineer was a faint wave of his black tail as he crawled slowly over a snowy mass wedged far down in the recesses of the frozen chasm, apparently unhurt but hopelessly unable ever to return. And there we had to leave him, another victim to the dangerous habit of climbing alone and of venturing upon a glacier without a rope!*

Near the end of its Yoho Valley sojourn, the Outram and Whymper party visited the lower valley of the Yoho to see Twin Falls. Outram ran into a "crowd" of tourists, guests of Edward Duchesnay, assistant general superintendent of the Western Division of the railway. Duchesnay had some high-powered guests with him, including amateur glaciologist George Vaux and his daughter, Mary. Mary would later become the third wife of Charles Doolittle Walcott, the secretary of the Smithsonian and discoverer of the most famous fossils in the world — the Cambrian fossils of the Burgess Shales above Emerald Lake. The party gathered to witness the spectacle of two swollen streams falling in tandem over the 100 metre wall above them. To their great disappointment, however, one of the falls had been blocked by a rock slide and had stopped flowing. The obliging Duchesnay instantly dispatched workmen to remove the obstruction so that his distinguished guests could view the falls at their best. Under Outram's later recommendation, Mt. Duchesnay and Duchesnay Lake would be named for this friendly, considerate man. This, however, would not be the last time one of the Twin Falls stopped. Nearly 50 years later park warden Glen Brook had to clear one of the upper channels to allow the wonder to continue.

After three weeks in the regions of the Upper Yoho, Whymper and his party returned to Field. The ever-ambitious Outram went almost immediately on two other expeditions, both of them to the Goodsirs in the Ottertail Range. Both attempts to climb the Goodsirs were unsuccessful, adding significantly to the reputation of the mountain in contemporary climbing circles. For all his efforts, Outram had to be satisfied with a good look at the Goodsirs and the Ice River Valley, where he noted with interest a radical change in geology from the main ranges of the Rockies— there was sodalite, a mineral found in igneous rock, in the bed of the Ice River. The Ice River possesses the only igneous rock outcroppings in Yoho. These outcroppings were formed when molten materials from deep in the earth's core intruded into the sedimentary rock during mountain building. Molten material flowed into cracks and fissures at the bases of new mountains, which were formed as the ancient seafloor was shattered and uplifted. Outram also noted the presence of syenite, a form of igneous rock formed largely of aluminum silicates and potassium, sodium, calcium, or barium. Sodalite, for which the Ice River is particularly well known, is a translucent blue sodium aluminum silicate of striking beauty. There are places along the Ice River where the riverbed is composed almost entirely of this beautiful stone. Outram's powers of observation and apparent knowledge of geology are as remarkable as his writing:

Far up, the valley-head is closed abruptly by a wall of cliffs, down which the gleaming, broken waters of several picturesque cascades leap from ledge to ledge, like threads and bands of silver, from the upper slopes of snow and glistening parapet of ice that crowns the whole and acts as sponsor to the river and its valley-bed.

Another interest of this small but fascinating gem of Nature's handiwork is found in its peculiar formation from a geological point of view. Almost alone and to by far the greatest extent, so far as is at present known, amongst the hosts of ranges in the Canadian Rocky Mountain chain, the Ottertail Group provides exception to the prevailing Middle Cambrian to Lower Carboniferous strata, and here a belt of syenite runs right athwart the centre of the limestone mass from east to west, severed itself by the sudden cleavage of the Ice River Valley.

Considerable mineral wealth is likely to be stored within the rocky treasure-house of these everlasting hills; zinc, mica, sodalite, and the richer ores have already yielded their quota to the miner. It is also a good region for the sportsman; the woods that clothe the lower slopes, the bleaker ridges, and the *broken crags, harbour the bear and deer and offer advantageous haunts for mountain goats, whilst silvery trout gleam in the streams below.*

While Outram was in the Ice River Valley trying to climb the Goodsir Towers and rhapsodizing about minerals and silvery trout, Edward Whymper was on a blowout in Field with outfitter and guide Jimmy Simpson. If Whymper was a drinker, he had met his match in Simpson. This is Simpson's account of the story. It is debatable whether anyone could "get" Simpson drunk; he was the kind of cowboy who could do that all by himself. Still, Simpson makes some insightful observations of the great English climber:

Whymper was peculiar, possibly because he had been lionized too much, but he was so determined an individual and such a strong character that he resembled a bulldog very much like the cartoons of that dog standing astride the Union Jack ready to devour anyone who touched it.

He got me very drunk at the old Field Hotel after the camp was over and confided that he had a very clever brother who drank himself to death and said he, "Yes, Simpson, very clever and I often used to say to him 'George, why don't you take it in moderation the same as I do.'" You know what moderation he used.....

A Park for the People

The growing success of railway promotion rapidly increased the number of visitors to the Canadian Rockies. More people came to be employed locally by the railroad, and others moved West in great numbers to colonize the newly opened frontier. A fledgling national parks service gradually grew to take greater responsibility for the land entrusted to its care. The expansion of Yoho's boundary in 1901 and the expansion of Banff National Park westward rekindled concern about the potential threat of private development to the protected status of these new reserves. The lesson of Niagara Falls still lingered in the political winds. For a formative period in the history of national parks, western parks benefitted greatly from being run by Ottawa in the distant, heavily populated east.

In 1896, 44-year-old Howard Douglas became the second superintendent of Banff National Park. Early in his stint at Banff, a controversy arose about hunting in the national park preserves. Since hunting contributed to the reputation and economic development of the area, the first superintendent of Banff, George Stewart, had not discouraged big-game hunting outside protected areas. Howard Douglas, however, had been exposed to the new environmental philosophies of transcendental American writers and thinkers like John Muir through discussion with well-educated tourist-mountaineers who had been visiting the Rockies since the railway opened. He noted that the publicity generated

Wapta Lodge was originally accessible only by canoe or steam launch from a rail siding on the other side of Summit or Wapta Lake. (Photo courtesy of the Whyte Museum of the Canadian Rockies.)

by these writers was bringing a sophisticated brand of visitor to Banff. As a result, even during a depression, Banff was attracting more visitors than Yellowstone was. Educated classes were lamenting the near-extinction of the buffalo and the threat to the existence of many other species of wildlife. Although hunting inside the mountain parks had been prohibited since 1890, Douglas knew that it regularly took place inside park boundaries.

To protect the wildlife, Douglas began a successful lobby to increase the area of each of the mountain parks and to introduce game wardens into the national park system. Douglas did not like the idea of employing local people as wardens. Although he was forced to do so for many years, he hardly trusted them. "They are inclined to wink at breaches of the law," he noted, "rather than incur the enmity of their neighbours." Douglas was later able to help form the Fire and Game Guardian Service, the parent organization of today's Warden Service. In association with the creation of a stewardship role for wardens in Yoho, official park records name Douglas as its first superintendent in 1905. In 1906, the office of the superintendent was filled locally in Field by C. D. Hoar, and the park's first warden, Roxy Hamilton, came to work in Yoho. The bases for enduring protection of the park were now, at last, in place. A few decades of mining and logging, however, would have to be tolerated before the Parks Service would gain any real control over Yoho. In the meantime, visitors from all over the world continued to flock to the wonder that was Yoho, and the last of its unclimbed peaks were scaled.

The First Ascent of Yoho's Twin Giants

By 1909 the Goodsir Towers were among the last of the serious mountaineering challenges south of the main line of the Canadian Pacific Railway.

The Goodsirs are the two highest peaks in the massif between the Ottertail and Ice River valleys in Yoho National Park. The twin towers of the mountain were named in 1858 by Dr. James Hector for John Goodsir, who was a professor of anatomy at Edinburgh University, and his brother,

H. D. S. Goodsir, who was an assistant surgeon on the last and fatal Franklin expedition. There is plenty of room for both names on the mountain, for the towers are immense.

They are also forbidding and difficult to climb. One of the earliest references to the mountain was made by surveyor J. J. McArthur in his report to the Minister of the Interior in 1887. McArthur had just begun the base surveys of the mountainous terrain that bulged up around the thin railway belt holding up the pants of this adolescent nation. McArthur considered the Goodsirs a triad and referred to their summits as the Three Sister Peaks. At that time, the Goodsirs were the highest mountains yet to be surveyed south of the line of the railroad. McArthur also noted that they were probably higher than peaks north of the rail line too, at least until one reached the giants that reared up at the headwaters of the Athabasca near the Columbia Icefield. The south tower of the mountain was particularly impressive, looming up with a lonely remoteness to an altitude somewhere around 3350 metres. It was this peak that Charles Fay, president of the Appalachian Mountain Club, noticed during his first visit to the Canadian Alps in 1890. The first mountaineer to visit the Ice River valley was J. Henry Scattergood, in 1900. The following year, Scattergood and Fay went together to the Ice River with James Outram with the intention of making the first ascent of the mountain. Their guide was Christian Hasler.

The Fay-Scattergood-Outram expedition to the Goodsirs in 1901 was undertaken with the assistance of packer Ross Peecock. While Peecock was establishing a camp at the Ice River, Christian Hasler led Fay, Scattergood, and Outram from the railway bridge over Ottertail Creek to a bivouac at timberline near the headwaters of Haskins Creek, just below a major cleft on the back of Mt. Hurd. On the following day they advanced from their high camp to make the first ascent of Mt. Vaux. From its summit they were able to reconnoitre the shoulder of the south tower of the Goodsirs, upon which they hoped to advance the next day.

In 1901 the upper Ice River was a real wilderness, much as it is today. Only a few prospectors had even seen the valley, and Fay and his friends were the first party to attempt to climb the mountain. Since it was clear that a one-day assault would be inadequate to guarantee success on such a big mountain, a bivouac was established between two gnarled alpine fir trees at the base of a spur of the southern tower. As Fay described it, the sun set clear, the stars gleamed above them with a joyous brightness, and the climbers fell asleep with the idea that these were signs that they would soon be victors over the untamed monster at whose feet they dared to lie so serenely. Unfortunately, things did not work out quite as Fay expected they would.

83

After passing the last evidence of prospectors in the high valley, the climbers made their way up the lowest flanks of the first ridge south of their bivouac. There they began their first real climbing. At 3048 metres, where the ridge joined another ridge striking more to the south, they paused for a second breakfast. Soon they were at the major obstacle of the climb — a corniced arête connected to a steep snow shoulder. The climbers were successful in making the dangerous move over the arête and to the top of a steep cliff that connected directly to the summit. It was here that Christian Hasler made the decision that saved their lives. Charles Fay tells us what it was like just below the summit of the south tower of the Goodsirs on that fearful summer day in 1901:

A most ominous situation revealed itself. The final peak was before us, and its summit hardly three hundred feet distant — a great white hissing mass, — precipice on the hidden left side, a steep snowslope of perhaps 65 to 70 degrees on the right. Under the July sun its whole surface was seemingly in a state of flux, slipping over the underlying mass with a constant, threatening hiss. A second narrow arête led across to this final summit. This, too, was corniced, and in a remarkable way. The swirl of the wind had produced an unusual spectacle. At the beginning and at the end, the cornice hung out to the right; in the middle, a reversed section of it overhung the abyss on the left. The two smaller ones could doubtless have been passed. To cross the middle of the section meant trusting ourselves to the sun-beaten slope already in avalanching condition. Indeed, while we studied it, and as if to furnish the final argument to our debate, the snow on our right impinging against the cornice, well back upon which Hasler was standing, broke away, and down went a well-developed avalanche a couple of thousand feet over that much-tilted surface, and vanished in sheer plunge that landed it perhaps three thousand feet below that. It was a suggestive and persuasive sight. Feeling sure that we had seen enough for one day, we beat a careful retreat.

Although Fay was anxious to get even for his defeat on the giant Goodsir, this opportunity did not come for two more years. Early in the summer of 1903, Fay received a telegram from his friend Herschel Parker, who had just returned to Field from an attempt to scale the mountain with Christian Kaufmann and Christian Hasler as his guides. Their ascent had been thwarted by a heavy snowfall that blocked their way to the summit at very nearly the altitude the Fay party had been forced to turn back in 1901. Parker and the guides were waiting for the snow to melt to make another attempt, and Parker wondered if Fay would like to get on the next train west to join them. Fay did just that. Within only a few days, Fay had joined Parker, Kaufmann, and Hasler, and a bivouac had been established below the peak. Kaufmann reported a few hours later that snow had begun to fall, and when the climbers awoke at dawn, they were enveloped in a perfect winter. With the assistance of packer Walter Nixon, the party supplied itself for a siege. While waiting for the snow to melt from the big summit, the climbers amused themselves by making the ascent of "Little Goodsir," the smallest of the Goodsir triad, a mountain now known as Sentry Peak. The expedition then made one more attempt on the mountain. The snow remained in perfect condition for the entire day, and when the climbers reached the final ridge, they noticed that although the summit arête was covered with snow, there were no cornices. They gingerly crossed the narrow arête, the sides of the mountain falling nearly vertically into the abyss on either side. At eleven o'clock in the morning on July 16, 1903, Parker, Fay, Hasler, and Kaufmann became the first to stand on the summit of the giant south tower of Goodsir.

There was still another tower to climb, however. Only a few metres shorter than the south tower, the north peak of the Goodsir is a fearsome obstacle in its own right. This tower was first attempted by Dr. August Eggers, of Grand Forks, North Dakota, in the summer of 1903. Although Eggers was an accomplished climber who made the first ascents of Mt. Biddle and Deltaform Peak, he and his guides, Hans and Christian Kaufmann, were prevented from reaching the summit by yet another of the snowstorms that plague this peak. Eggers and his guides clearly understood that the high altitude of this immense tower meant more severe weather and the potential for deteriorating climbing conditions. They were within 300 or 400 metres of the summit before they turned back. Even at that, they had severe difficulty in getting off the mountain and reaching their camp. As is the way with mountaineers, however, Eggers was not finished with the Goodsirs. His defeat only made him more adamant about succeeding on the very difficult summit of the north tower. The mountain would test him severely.

It was not until August of 1909, after the Annual Camp of the Alpine Club of Canada at nearby Lake O'Hara had broken up, that Eggers once again had an opportunity to attempt another first ascent. While prominent members of the British Alpine Club were charging around the Yoho Valley with A. O. Wheeler, Dr. Eggers invited Canadians J. P. Forde and P. D. McTavish, among others, to join an exploratory party to the upper regions of the Ice River. Forde, who worked with the railway, was an experienced climber from Revelstoke, and his friend P. D. McTavish was an ambitious climber from Vancouver. They had begun climbing together in the Coast Mountains and were now testing themselves against the more accessible peak of the interior of British Columbia. Although most of the party was interested only in examining the beautiful valley, Eggers made it clear that he intended to climb the north tower of the Goodsirs and to this end invited Édouard Feuz as his guide.

In a very sportsmanlike and gentlemanly way, Forde and McTavish were reluctant to take Eggers up on his offer. After all, it was Eggers's mountain, if only by virtue of this earlier very daring effort to reach its summit. Nevertheless, they accepted the invitation and the climb was begun early on the morning of August 16, 1909. The climbers left their camp on the shores of the

Ice River at 5:08 am (Forde was precise in his record keeping). By 7:00 am, the small expedition reached the wall of the mountain and began a southerly traverse across the western face of the peak. By 10:00 am, they had reached the long southwesterly ridge that runs down to the Ice River, where they discovered they could have taken this ridge direct from camp and saved themselves much time in the ascent. It was at this time that Forde and McTavish realized why Eggers had been so insistent on their joining his party. The fact of the matter was that Eggers was hardly in condition to make a serious ascent of the mountain. Not only was Eggers unfit, he was also unwell. But he would not think of giving up, at least until he had expended every ounce of effort in getting as far as he could up his mountain.

The climbers stayed to the ridge they had discovered until it broke off into steep cliffs. They then traversed a long rock slide on the south side of the peak, at the top of which they found another ridge immediately between the north and south towers. It was here that a large rock was put into quick downward motion by one of the climbers. No one noticed until much later that the rock had completely sliced the rope and that it was held together by only one or two strands. By 2:00 pm, the climbers were at the base of the north tower. Here Eggers gave out and determined to wait for the rest of the team to make the ascent as best they could. Forde, McTavish, and Feuz traversed the base of the tower along the upper reaches of a V of snow that forms a prominent route marker on the mountain during the summer months. This traverse brought them to a snow couloir, and they zigzagged over very uncertain terrain to the summit. Since smoke from forest fires filled every valley, the views were poor, an omen, perhaps, that the mountain was far from finished with them, even though they had reached its summit. It was already 4:00 pm. They were worried that they would be benighted on the shoulders of this giant, and that is exactly what came to pass.

It took the climbers more than two hours to descend to where Eggers was waiting for them. By then darkness was already beginning to fall. Their strategy was to follow the southwesterly ridge as far as they could with the idea of reaching timberline, from which they could reach their camp by lamplight. By 10:00 pm, they found themselves rappelling off cliff faces into total darkness. Clearly, there was a real risk of death, which Feuz undoubtedly brought to their attention. Reluctantly, they chose to bivouac on a small ledge to wait for the dawn. At 6:30 am, Forde reached camp ahead of Eggers and Feuz after 25 hours on the mountain. Although Forde does not say so directly, it had been a terrifying night and the climbers were lucky to be alive. Such was the confidence of the members of the party in the Ice River Valley below that they did not worry at all about their friends stranded on the mountain. J. P. Forde describes the welcome the climbers received after their triumphant first ascent of the north tower:

*Edward Feuz was one of the greatest moun-
taineers and guides to have ever lived in
Canada. His name is very closely associated
with Yoho and, in particular, Lake O'Hara
where he guided many successful climbs. In
this photograph we see Edward enjoying the
summit of Cathedral Mountain in Yoho.
(Photo courtesy of the Whyte Museum of
the Canadian Rockies.)*

*Our desire to reach camp was not on our own account at all, but to
relieve the anxiety of our friends, whom we had pictured as sitting around the
fire all night, talking, with bated breath and white, drawn faces, of what terrible sufferings we must be enduring, and our disgust may be imagined when
we found them sleeping, and to add insult to injury, snoring most heartily.
However, they were all very glad to see us back, and to know that another of
the now very few unclimbed peaks of note in the better known portion of the
Rockies had been struck off the list. As soon as we reached camp one of the
guides started off with horses for Dr. Eggers and Feuz, who rode in, ready for
breakfast, about 8:30 am.*

We can surmise from Forde's remark that there was a great deal of competi-
tion to climb the remaining Canadian giants and that the status came not from
taking the most difficult routes to the summit but from simply making the summit by any means at all. There was a bit of summit-bagging going on here —
some climbers were beginning to choose their mountains not for reason of sport
and challenge but simply because they had not been climbed before. This was
easy to do now that the preliminary exploration had been done and the first
maps had been made. It is perhaps telling that only two hours after Forde and
McTavish reached the camp, the guide Rudolph Aemmer arrived with a party
of two Americans who were very disappointed to find the mountain already
climbed. One of the Americans was Herschel Parker, who went on from this
disappointing development to make the first ascent a few days later of yet
another giant, Mt. Hungabee. Hungabee straddles the Great Divide between
Paradise Valley near Lake Louise on the east and the Opabin Plateau and Lake
O'Hara in Yoho on the west. It was to this area of highly concentrated wonder
that visitor interest would gradually shift as the next phase in the history of
Yoho began to unfold.

Lake O'Hara is one of the most special places in all of the Rockies. Rock, snow, ice, water, sky and light meet there to create a sense of intimate sense of place like no other.

Chapter 5

Lake O'Hara: Wonder Concentrated

W hen people state that they have been to Lake O'Hara they could mean a number of things. They could mean that they rode the bus from the parking lot at the junction of Highway 1A and the Trans-Canada near the Great Divide over the 12 kilometres of gravel and potholes up Cataract Brook to the lake to visit the lodge that sits on its shore. Here one may spend hours just taking in the view of the dazzling teal-green lake, which, in the mornings and evenings, is often still enough to reflect Mts. Victoria and Lefroy. Together they form the back wall of a great stone bowl, with Seven Veil Falls spilling over it to form the lake.

But "Lake O'Hara" is more than just this lake. It is the gentle trail that circles the lake. It is also the steep switchbacks that lead up to grand views at Wiwaxy Gap. Wiwaxy Gap is the starting point of an even greater adventure, for here begins the mountaineering route up the Huber Ledges to the western route on Mt. Victoria. "Lake O'Hara" is also the elegant, moderately graded stone walkway past rumbling waterfalls and a series of tiny lakelets to Lake Oesa. Because of its high altitude, Lake Oesa is covered with ice well into the summer. "Lake O'Hara" also includes the high alpine route from Oesa over the impressive ledges on the shoulder of Mt. Yukness to Opabin Lake and the Opabin Plateau. At the head of the Opabin Plateau is the alpine route to Opabin Pass, a glacier-shrouded shoulder from which mountaineers make their way down to the Eagle's Aeries and up to Wenkchemna Pass and Moraine Lake in Banff National Park.

"Lake O'Hara" is much more than even the remarkable stillness of Opabin Lake set ablaze in the spring light with the green fire of larch trees. Yet another manicured trail leads, by way of carefully laid flagstones, to the lip of the plateau. From here it is possible to return by a series of switchbacks, past more waterfalls back to Lake O'Hara. From a viewpoint on this lip, known as Opabin Prospect, one can see that there are other lakes in the upper Cataract Brook valley besides Lake O'Hara. Fed by rain and the melting of snow rather than by the melting of glacial ice, these lakes are greener than Lake O'Hara.

From the same prospect, a whole other domain included in the O'Hara area can be seen to the west. The Odaray Plateau is a great swatch of larch forest that glows like faint green fire in the spring, then burns yellow gold after being touched by the frost in the fall. In a small meadow in the midst of this larch forest are two small cabins that belong to the Alpine Club of Canada, the country's oldest mountaineering organization. A trail wanders past them and then forks south toward McArthur Pass and west toward the head of the Odaray Plateau. The McArthur Pass trail is also considered part of the Lake O'Hara area. After leaving Elizabeth Parker hut, named for the club's co-founder and first secretary, the trail winds through wildflowers and huge larches and past a series of shallow pools before climbing gently to the boulder strewn pass. From the summit of the pass, the trail forks again. One fork leads down McArthur Creek into some of Yoho's wildest country, and the other leads upward through some interesting cliff bands to the lip of a cirque that cradles Lake McArthur, easily one of the most beautiful places anywhere in the mountain world. In looking once again at the map, you can see that Lake O'Hara has a lot of mountain scenery jammed into a small but very accessible area. The sheer diversity of mountain features creates a unique sense of place.

Of all the places in the Canadian West that leave a lasting impression on visitors, Lake O'Hara is one of the most remarkable. Few other places in the Rockies overwhelm people the way Lake O'Hara does. Lake Louise might affect the visitors in the same way if it were not so near a highway and did not always have so many people gawking from its shores. Tonquin Valley in Jasper has a hint of that Lake O'Hara feeling, but it is a big wall view that overwhelms in a way that is out of all human scale. Floe Lake in Kootenay National Park with its great rock wall is stunning but doesn't emanate that same intense sense of place that O'Hara is so famous for. Even Emerald Lake does not offer the intimacy of experience that one feels while in the amphitheatre of peaks that surround O'Hara's shores. Its clear lakes and dazzling waterfalls, impressive Great Divide peaks, luxuriant plateaus and alpine meadows, high walking trail circuits, mind-slowing vistas, and fascinating history make Lake O'Hara the wonder of wonders in Yoho.

Although the main peaks of the Great Divide were explored from the east by way of Lake Louise much earlier, Lake O'Hara was not discovered by Europeans until James McArthur found his way to it via Cataract Brook in the summer of 1890. The lake was later named for retired Lieutenant Colonel Robert O'Hara, who was among the earliest visitors to the lake. During his explorations, McArthur also crossed a nearby pass and climbed into the amphitheatre occupied by another stunning lake, which was eventually to bear his name.

Samuel Allen and the Back Door to Yoho

If McArthur had not discovered Lake O'Hara in the summer of 1890, it would have very likely been discovered by Samuel Allen. Although largely overshadowed by his friend Walter Wilcox, who wrote two books on early

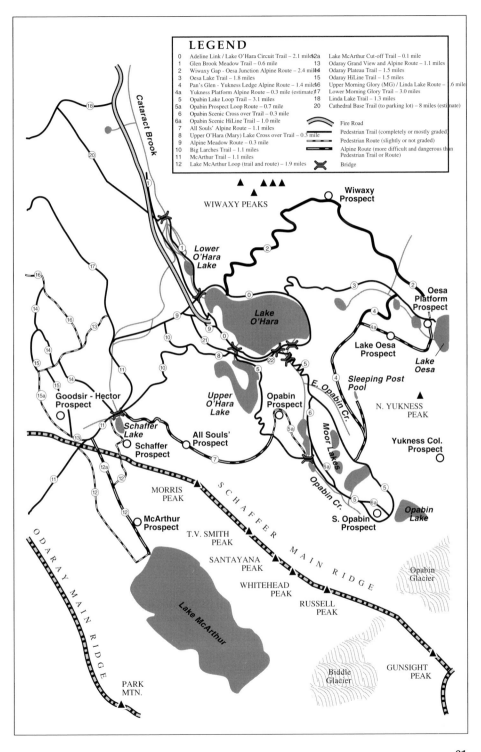

LEGEND

0	Adeline Link / Lake O'Hara Circuit Trail – 2.1 miles	12a	Lake McArthur Cut-off Trail – 0.1 mile
1	Glen Brook Meadow Trail – 0.6 mile	13	Odaray Grand View and Alpine Route – 1.1 miles
2	Wiwaxy Gap - Oesa Junction Alpine Route – 2.4 miles	14	Odaray Plateau Trail – 1.5 miles
3	Oesa Lake Trail – 1.8 miles	15	Odaray HiLine Trail – 1.5 miles
4	Pan's Glen – Yukness Ledge Alpine Route – 1.4 miles	16	Upper Morning Glory (MG) / Linda Lake Route – .6 mile
4a	Yukness Platform Alpine Route – 0.3 mile (estimate)	17	Lower Morning Glory Trail – 3.0 miles
5	Opabin Lake Loop Trail – 3.1 miles	18	Linda Lake Trail – 1.3 miles
5a	Opabin Prospect Loop Route – 0.7 mile	20	Cathedral Base Trail (to parking lot) – 8 miles (estimate)
6	Opabin Scenic Cross over Trail – 0.3 mile		
6a	Opabin Scenic HiLine Trail – 1.0 mile		Fire Road
7	All Souls' Alpine Route – 1.1 miles		Pedestrian Trail (completely or mostly graded)
8	Upper O'Hara (Mary) Lake Cross over Trail – 0.3 mile		Pedestrian Route (slightly or not graded)
9	Alpine Meadow Route – 0.3 mile		Alpine Route (more difficult and dangerous than
10	Big Larches Trail – 1.1 miles		Pedestrian Trail or Route)
11	McArthur Trail – 1.1 miles		Bridge
12	Lake McArthur Loop (trail and route) – 1.9 miles		

exploration in the Rockies, Allen contributed a great deal to the exploration of the Lake Louise area of the Great Divide. A philogist, he sought every opportunity to learn the names of places used by the Natives and applied them to the maps he made of the Moraine Lake and Lake O'Hara areas.

Allen came to know about the Canadian Rockies in a rather circuitous way. His mother had been a part of a group of American visitors who travelled by train through the Rockies in 1889. The eclectic group she travelled with included amateur glaciologists George and William Vaux, their sister Mary (later Mary Vaux Walcott), and her friend Mary Townsend Sharples (later Mary Schaffer). Mrs. Allen returned to Philadelphia and shared her enthusiasm for the Rockies with her son, Samuel, then a freshman at Yale. A bright, active, and alert scholar of languages, he was intrigued by his mother's descriptions of the beautiful Rockies and made a vow to visit them.

Allen first came to the Rockies in the summer of 1891, when he toured the West by train, visiting Glacier House, Emerald Lake, and Field. Above the village of Field, Allen and a companion had searched the slopes for trilobite fossils. His companion on that short but very steep walk grieved for the little town huddled at the base of the canyon peaks. The town in the 1880s had been "a luxuriant garden, a bower of ferns and moss." But a forest fire had since scarred the valley, and only young pines relieved the terrible scars left behind by the blaze.

It was not until 1893 that Allen made his second visit to the Great Divide.

Named for the great surveyor and climber, J.J. McArthur, McArthur Lake can be reached by way of a beautiful trail from Lake O'Hara.

By this time he had teamed up with Walter Dwight Wilcox, a recent graduate of Yale who had serious interests in both geology and photography. Allen had high ambitions for this visit. He wanted to climb Mt. Victoria, which at that time was still known as Mt. Green. The mountain proved to be more than the young climbers could handle, however. On their first attempt from the Lake Louise side, they were stopped by crevasses on the lower glacier. For their second attempt, they used a route that skirted the bases of the mountains now called Mt. Collier and Pope's Peak. Approaching the base of Mt. Victoria, the climbers were greeted by thundering ice avalanches that fell from the Upper Victoria Glacier. The rumbling ice fell into the col that connected Mt. Victoria with Mt. Lefroy. Allen named the route from the lower glacier to the top of the col the Death Trap and correctly surmised that both Victoria and Lefroy could be climbed from the summit of the col. But Allen and Wilcox had to be satisfied with a good reconnaissance of the mountain, for the Death Trap was too much for them. Allen had to wait until the next year to climb to the summit of that col to what is now Abbot Pass. When at last he made that ascent, it was from the west, from Lake O'Hara, which he discovered by a completely different route.

Allen and Wilcox returned from their 1893 expedition raving about the glories of the Canadian Rockies. The successes and failures of their expedition had greatly affected both of them, and it was not long before they were planning for the next season of exploring, mountaineering, and surveying in the mountains of the Great Divide. In 1894, their expedition was expanded. Joining Allen and Wilcox were George Warrington, Louis Frissell, and Yandall Henderson. Instead of two inexperienced mountaineers, there were now five. They relied heavily on a "how to" book on climbing published by the Badminton Library for advice on how to overcome some of the major rock and ice features that stood in the way of their enthusiastic rush for the peaks.

While Wilcox, Frissell, and Henderson were awaiting the later arrival of Allen and Warrington at Lake Louise, Wilcox led a disastrous attempt on Mt. Lefroy that caused Frissell to be quite badly injured. By the time that Warrington and Allen arrived two weeks later, Frissell was still on crutches. More than that, however, an unspoken tension had developed around the leadership of the party. Perhaps because of his strong leadership after Frissell's accident and the creation of a close climbing unit born of the Lefroy adventure, Wilcox appeared to hold greater sway over the ad hoc expedition. Allen was increasingly at odds with his companions. There were arguments about place names and the location of peaks on their maps. There were disagreements about the routes that should be taken Throughout, Allen continued his careful study of native names, applying them where he could to the developing map of the Lake Louise area. The distance between Allen and his companions continued to grow. It was this friction between Allen and the others that would lead to the discovery of the back door to Yoho and the Lake O'Hara area.

The party discovered the Valley of the Ten Peaks, and Allen named each of the summits after native words for the numbers one to ten. The explorers had also discovered Wenkchemna Pass at the head of the Valley of the Ten Peaks and had crossed the pass into the head of Prospectors Valley. By this time friction between them was becoming palpable. Allen, who wanted to return to the west side of Wenkchemna Pass, could find no one who wanted to go with him. Much against the advice of his companions, Allen decided to make the trip by himself. Leaving very early in the morning, Allen crossed Wenkchemna Pass and proceeded to the Eagle's Aerie, a rocky, treeless valley made desolately beautiful by fantastically shaped rock formations. Advancing to the next col, which he named Opabin Pass, after the Stoney word for "rocky," he came to a glacier. Since it was still early in the day, Allen continued on the gentle ice to the névé. By 10:00 am, Allen was looking into what is now Yoho National Park. He was stunned by the view:

Before me I saw a broad valley, destitute of vegetation, and walled on either side by lofty, precipitous cliffs, the glaciers at the feet of which resembled the dashing waves of a stormy sea. From my feet downward swept the névé, terminating in a fine glacier below, while two lakes appeared in the rocky valley, for the sake of uniformity I have known as the Opabin Lakes.

The mountain on his left he named Mt. Biddle for his friend Anthony Joseph Drexel Biddle of Philadelphia. The mountain on his right he named Mt. Ringrose for A. E. L. Ringrose, a British traveller he had met in the Rockies. Two other peaks were partially visible on his right. One he named for the Swiss climber Emil Huber, who with Carl Sulzer had made the first ascent of Mt. Sir Donald at Rogers Pass on July 26, 1890. The other was the back of Mt. Victoria, and it was the sight of this mountain that gave Allen the idea to revisit this area to see if the Death Trap col could be climbed from the west side of the divide.

After making the first ascent of Mt. Temple, Allen decided to continue his explorations on the west side of the divide, hoping once again to find a way to the summit of the Death Trap col. Taking a 3:00 am train to Hector siding, Allen began a gradual ascent of Cataract Brook. Travelling upstream through the forest, Allen passed the cataract and the Watch Tower and then followed a smaller fork of a stream now known as Wiwaxy Creek to the lip of a hanging valley, where a blast of wind almost knocked him over. This hanging valley he called the Gorge of the Winds. This ample amount of exploration was enough for one day, and he returned to the tracks and more comfortable lodgings at Lake Louise with the idea of making one more journey up Cataract Brook.

After spending a day resting and making preparations for a return trip, Allen was foiled in his attempt to cross the Divide by high waters on Bath Creek. Just as Tom Wilson and Major Albert Rogers had experienced years before, meltwater from the Bath Glacier had swollen the creek, making it impossible to cross even on horseback. The next day Allen took himself and his

Samuel Allen near Opabin Pass in the summer of 1894. (Photo courtesy of the Whyte Museum of the Canadian Rockies.)

gear to Hector Siding by train. It was here that he met Yule Carryer, a University of Toronto–schooled Native who worked with the CPR in Field. By the afternoon, Allen and his companion once again reached the Gorge of the Winds, where they named the first prominent peak Wiwaxy, which Allen knew meant "windy" in Stoney. After climbing a scree slope so that they could overlook the valley, they decided to camp for the night. According to Allen, they made:

> ... *A resting place in a hollow of the heather slope, whence at a glance we could survey the valley beneath, with its lakes and river and peaks and glacier beyond, while the wind in the tamarack boughs made harmony with the music of the waterfall.*

Rising early the next morning, Allen and Carryer continued their climb into the hanging valley, where they discovered, according to Allen, "as beautiful a lake as I have ever seen." Allen named it for Colonel O'Hara, who he believed had already sung its praises. (Although O'Hara left no known accounts of his explorations, it appears that he travelled extensively in the Rockies in 1894, when he apparently met Allen, and again in 1895.) Following the left shore,

Allen and Carryer were able to find a gully that allowed them access to the cliffs at the head of the lake. There they found another smaller lake at the base of a very sharp peak, which Allen named Yukness, the Stoney word for "sharp." After passing Yukness Lake, Allen came upon one of the grandest places in the Canadian Rockies, one of the most splendid scenes in all of Yoho — the Oesa basin:

The grey quartzite lay in slabs before us, level as a floor and polished by ancient ice. From the grooves and cracks of this ancient pavement grew long grass, as in the streets of some deserted city. As we stopped upon its surface our hot faces were cooled by a whiff from the ice-fields, and before us, the grey pavement gently sloping to meet it, lay a placid lake, a dark blue circle of about 1/2 mile in diameter.

Allen named the partially ice-covered shocking blue lake after the Stoney word for "ice." Lake Oesa lay at the base of a huge scree slope that rose to a col high above, between the back shoulders of Mt. Victoria and Mt. Lefroy. Allen had discovered the west side of the Death Trap col, the pass that was to be later named for Phillip Stanley Abbot, who died in an attempt to be the first to climb Lefroy. After spending the night near the shores of Yukness Lake, Allen and Carryer made the first ascent of the pass. As anyone who has ever attempted the pass from the west will attest, the scree and talus slopes make for frustrating climbing. Yule Carryer was actually the first to the summit. Allen explains:

Soon I was obliged to take to the ledges of the cliff. There was not far to climb. A foothold, a couple of handholds, a wriggle, a moment of doubt, and I was poised upon a fine ledge, whence ascent to the col was less difficult. Carryer had found easier work on the right side, and was awaiting me on the summit.

Allen had virtually circled the great massive of mountains that form the great divide separating Lake Louise from Lake O'Hara. Standing on the 2923 metre summit, Allen connected his explorations with those he and Wilcox had made the previous year. The next day he and Carryer climbed to the col now known as Wiwaxy Gap, which Allen called "the most consummate view, from an artistic view, that I have ever seen in the Rockies." Already the reputation of the O'Hara region was beginning to grow.

The Legend Grows

Although relations between Samuel Allen and Walter Wilcox had been strained during their expedition to the Rockies in the summer of 1894, Wilcox was duly impressed by Allen's description of the Lake O'Hara area. In the late summer of 1896, Wilcox visited the lake with Tom Wilson. Three years later Wilcox returned, with Ross Peecock to explore the upper reaches of the Vermilion and Otterhead watersheds. They arrived at Lake O'Hara after much difficult travel from where Highway 93 now runs through Kootenay National Park. Lake O'Hara was their last camp, and Wilcox enjoyed the experience very much. Even at that time, the trails in the Lake O'Hara area were much improved over many of those in other areas in Yoho. Tom Wilson had been right that Native peoples had made extensive use of the McArthur Pass area in crossing the main ranges of the Great Divide.

It was September 10, 1899. In the following passages, from The Rockies of Canada, G. P. Putman & Sons, New York, 1900, Wilcox describes the last camp of the season, and the trip over McArthur Pass, and what it was like to camp alone on the shores of Yoho's most famous lake:

he trail, after climbing some way, descends into a fine open valley, where we made very rapid time, by driving our horses up the clear stream, and crossing from side to side. In five miles we came to a side valley on our right,

The Opabin Plateau. High above Lake O'Hara, this small valley is one of the most stunning of all of Yoho's wonders.

which I long held in view as the one we should take. After countless delays in beating the trail, we found ourselves, as the daylight failed, at the top of a pass, where, on a single ridge of green, we were surrounded by apparently impassable rock-slides. Westward, the wan green sky was hung with ominous clouds, brooding over a mountain, which, like a massive pyramid, filled all the gap between the west and north. The trail was finally discovered over the rock-slide. Here the Indians had filled all the crevices between the stones with smaller ones, and paved a safe but narrow path among rough ledges. The south side of Mt. Victoria lay in plain view before us, and at 7:30 pm after ten hours of marching, we pitched our camp in the darkness beside O'Hara Lake. Our tent was on the identical spot where Wilson and I had slept on bare ground in the fall of 1896.

In the morning the chickadees were singing and calling to one another very sweetly among the spruces. The mosquitoes were as numerous as in summer, though the air was springlike. It was to be a day of rest after our long and tiresome marches, for we were now within six hours of the railroad. O'Hara Lake was a favourite resort of a gentleman of that name, who came here frequently some years ago, and was probably the first tourist to visit the place. If the six most beautiful lakes in the mountains were selected, this would certainly be among them. Personally, I regard Lake Louise, Moraine Lake, and O'Hara Lake as the three finest I have ever seen. Each is between one and two miles long and each has certain individual charms.

O'Hara Lake is surrounded by a noble amphitheatre, the cul-de-sac made by Mts. Victoria, Lefroy, and Hungabee. The water and even the bottom itself are coloured a vivid, clear green. Not far from the outlet, a pretty bay is made by a narrow point which projects a line of trees into the water. Then it dissolves in a chain of rocky islets, covered in part with moss, willows, a few dwarf spruces, and beds of purple-rayed asters. Beyond this miniature cape, the shore sweeps out into the broader reaches of the lake, and carries the eye to the cliffs of the farthest shore, where the inlet stream makes a curtain of water as it falls in cascades over dark rocks. At night and sometimes by day, you may hear the sound of water distinctly, a mile or more distant, as it is carried over the lake. I have never discovered whether there are any fish in this lake or not, though every condition is favourable to them.

The next day we marched six hours down the valley, over a bad trail, and reached the railroad at Hector. Here we traversed burnt timber for the first and only time, of our thirty-one days' trip. When near the valley end, a thunderstorm came up from the west, and swept a curtain of hail and rain over the mountains. A high waterfall on the side of Mt. Victoria was stopped and blown back against the cliffs by the strong winds. We left the wilderness and passed out of the mountains while the raging of storm and the roar of thunder bade us farewell.

The death of Phillip Abbot on the Death Trap side of Mt. Lefroy attracted considerable attention to the Canadian Rockies. In 1897, an international expedition that included some of the best mountaineers in Britain and the United States avenged the death of Abbot by making the first ascents of Mt. Lefroy and Mt. Victoria. In the summer of 1898, Professor Charles Fay, president of the Appalachian Mountain Club and a witness to Abbot's death, came back to the Rockies to build on the glories of the previous summer, when, as a member of the international team, he had at last climbed Mt. Lefroy. With Fay was Rest F. Curtis. Accompanied by a young cowboy named Jim Brewster, Fay and Curtis made the first traverse of Abbot Pass from Lake Louise to Lake O'Hara and back. While Brewster abandoned climbing to become a principle in the Brewster Transport Company, Fay became a mountaineering legend. In the summer of 1901 Fay repeated the Lake Louise – Lake O'Hara traverse with J. Henry Scattergood. They were accompanied on this expedition by James Outram, who had spent part of the summer with Edward Whymper in the upper Yoho Valley. Another member of this expedition was Nellie, a spaniel owned by the chef at Mt. Stephen House in Field. The three climbers heralded the little dog as "a splendid alpinist."

After accounts of such expeditions were published, it was clearly just a matter of time before the Lake O'Hara area became famous. The Alpine Club of Canada, created in 1906, realized the enormous climbing potential of the area. Now that more good maps were available, the last peaks along the main range of the Rockies were being climbed. With the ascent of the south tower of Mt. Goodsir in 1903 and the first ascent of Hungabee in 1908, the most challenging first ascents had been made. The drama of these ascents and the excellent Canadian Pacific Railway promotion made the area legendary. In 1909, when the Alpine Club of Canada held its third annual summer mountaineering camp in the meadows near the shores of Lake O'Hara, some of the best climbers in the world attended. Among them was the "Lion of the Matterhorn" himself, Sir Edward Whymper. Whymper, now a sad and lonely old man, was near the end of his life. Still troubled by the deaths of his companions on the famous descent of the Matterhorn in the summer of 1865, Whymper rose only once to a semblance of his old inspiration when he gave this speech at one of the nightly campfires:

Ladies and gentlemen, live, live, while you can. We're born to live, but born to die. Unite prudence with courage. Take heed to your steps lest you fall. Whatever you set your hands to do, do it with all your might. Act well your part, there all the honour lies. This, ladies and gentlemen, is the first, and it will be the last occasion on which I shall have the honour to speak to you. I came out from Europe expressly for this meeting, and tomorrow I start back. But, if I am unable to be with you in body, I shall, so long as I live, be with you in spirit, and wish you every success and prosperity.

The Alpine Club of Canada staged 13 camps at or near Lake O'Hara before the area became too well known and too heavily used to allow camps of that size to be held there. An interesting tradition that was started at the Lake O'Hara camps was an alpine journey of the five high passes of the area: from Abbot Pass to Mitre Pass to either Wastach or Sentinel Pass, then to Wenkchemna Pass and back over Opabin Pass to Lake O'Hara. Although the five pass route is not often taken today, at the turn of the 20th century it was considered one of the finest trips in all of the Rockies. Many claimed that more scenic mountain landscapes could be seen in two days on this journey than could be seen elsewhere in months.

John Singer Sargent at Lake O'Hara

In the early days of exploration in Yoho and the Lake O'Hara region, the beauty of the landscape was captured in paintings and drawings. Although photography had become quite sophisticated by 1900, colour film had not yet been invented. Hand-tinted lantern slides were in fairly common use for slide presentations, but the great bulk of large-scale advertising was done through colour reproduction of paintings and pen and ink sketches. As the beauty of Lake O'Hara became legendary, the lake and its environs began to attract some of North America's best-known painters. Among the first and finest of these was John Singer Sargent.

The son of an expatriate American physician and surgeon, John Singer Sargent was born in Florence, Italy, in January 1856. Sargent grew up almost without any formal education at all, preferring instead the rich and diverse instruction of the sophisticated social circles his family travelled in. Young John was a very bright boy. By the time that he was 20 and made his first visit back to the United States, Sargent was fluent in French, German, and Italian and was already being recognized for his precocious talent in art and music. In 1874, Sargent began studying painting in Paris under Charles-Émile-Auguste Duran, one of the most successful portrait artists of his time. After a highly productive period in Venice, where he lived and worked in close proximity to James Abbot McNeill Whistler and Henry James, Sargent had developed his painting skills to the highest European standards. Not only was Sargent a fine portrait painter, as he was soon to prove in the United States, he was also a very competent landscape painter who had developed a European style that could be readily adapted to new landscapes around the world. After a prolific period of portrait painting in the United States between 1887 and 1907, Sargent turned to large murals and landscape works. By the time that Sargent came to the Rockies in the summer of 1916, he was already one of the wealthiest and most famous painters in North America. To a man long used to wood-panelled estate rooms

The Warden cabin at Lake O'Hara is located on Sargent's point. John Singer Sargent was a famous society painter visited Lake O'Hara in the summer of 1916. He was one of America's foremost society painters.

and weekend hunting jaunts with the rich and famous, the shores of the lake were somewhat inhospitable. In time, however, the landscape made its way into Sargent's sensibility in a most profound way. In a letter to a relative, Sargent described his experience at the lake:

As I told you in my first or my last letter it was raining and snowing, my tent flooded, mushrooms sprouting in my boots, porcupines taking shelter in my clothes, canned food always fried in a black frying pan getting on my nerves, and a fine waterfall which was the attraction to the place pounding and thundering all night. I stood it for three weeks and yesterday came away with a repulsive picture. Now the weather has changed for the better and I am off again to try the simple (ach pfui) in tents at the top of another valley, this time with the gridiron instead of a frying pan and a perforated India rubber mat to stand on. It takes time to learn how to be really happy.

Despite the inconveniences, Sargent later reported to all and sundry that Lake O'Hara was the most beautiful lake he had ever seen in his life. This change of heart may have been inspired somewhat by the success of his painting of Lake O'Hara, which now resides at the Fogg Art Museum at Harvard University in Cambridge, Massachusetts. Certainly one of the finest landscape

101

paintings ever done in the Rockies, Sargent's 95 cm by 112 cm painting of the lake startles art critics even today. Despite the great force of his European training, the canvasses he painted at Lake O'Hara were remarkable in their faithfulness to place.

While Sargent was at Lake O'Hara, he camped on a small point on the lakeshore where the warden cabin now stands. This point is still known to many locals and regular visitors as Sargent's Point.

Other Painters

Some of Canada's greatest landscape painters also came to Lake O'Hara. Many of the earliest and finest Canadian painters were hired by the Canadian Pacific Railway to do promotional paintings of the Rockies.

Frederick Bell-Smith was among this group and was likely the first to paint Lake O'Hara. Born in London in 1846, Bell-Smith was the son of a portrait painter. He emigrated with his family to Montreal in 1866 and visited the Rockies in 1887. As a professional painter and photographer, Bell-Smith illustrated numerous newspaper and magazine articles for publications like the Canadian Illustrated News and Picturesque Canada.. Other important painters

Walter Phillips was an englishman who emigrated to Canada in 1913. Captured by the Canadian landscape, Phillips became one of the country's best watercolourists and wood-block print makers. This delicate woodcut of a falls below Lake Oesa was made in 1926. (Courtesy of the Glenbow Museum in Calgary, Alberta.)

who later became recognized as early Canadian masters include Lucius O'Brien, T. Mower Martin, and Marmaduke Matthews. These painters, however much they are associated with the Rockies, are not known to have painted in the Lake O'Hara area.

The next generation of famous Canadian painters is better represented in the long list of artists known to have visited Lake O'Hara. As principal founding member of Canada's Group of Seven, Lawren Harris had long advocated the role of art in defining a mystical union between the people of Canada and the Canadian landscape. Harris first visited the Rockies in 1924 and was later to visit the Lake Louise and Lake O'Hara regions often, especially after World War II, when he and his wife, Beth, moved to Vancouver. A. C. Leighton, a well-trained British watercolourist, worked on behalf of the railway during visits he made to the Rockies in 1925 and 1927. J. E. H. MacDonald, the oldest member of the Group of Seven, painted quite extensively in the O'Hara area, from 1926 until the early 1930s. He was often accompanied to O'Hara by Peter and Catharine Whyte, two prominent painters who lived in Banff. Since black and white photography could not always do justice to the Rockies, painting remained for decades the predominant way of expressing the grandeur of the Great Divide and the wonders of Yoho.

Building the Lake O'Hara Lodge

Despite the praise heaped on Yoho in the early days of the railway, visitors were slow to come even to magnificent places like Lake O'Hara. The central problem was one of accommodation. If you did not stay at Mt. Stephen House, there was no place for you to stay except in a tent carried along in a pack outfit by local guides. As rail traffic grew, the CPR realized that it had to expand the number of backcountry facilities to make the wilderness attractive. In the summer of 1913, the railway built the first log hut at Lake O'Hara. It was planned by the Swiss guides as a shelter for mountaineers who had crossed Abbot Pass and needed a place to stay while they climbed in the O'Hara area or perhaps continued on the five-pass route back to Lake Louise. The CPR did not apply to the park for a lease for the building until 1921 and probably would not have done so then were it not for the fact that the railway wanted to build two new chalets and additional teahouses at Lake O'Hara to provide space for the onslaught of tourists expected after the World War I was over. Records show that the first of the new chalets was to be built "where the CPR old camp is, on the trail between Lake O'Hara and Lake McArthur." The application for a temporary building permit and a leasehold of 0.4 hectare (1 acre) was made by Basil Gardom, chief of mountain hotel construction for the railway, to park superintendent F. N. Russell. The application further requested that the lease be expanded to 1.2 hectares (3 acres) should future visitor increases demand expansion of the property. Russell recommended the application to his superiors in Ottawa, arguing that the development "should prove quite an asset to the park." When Gardom's project was complete, the O'Hara camp comprised two cabins and five tents.

Gardom's application had been fortuitous. Lake O'Hara grew so quickly in popularity that the following year the railway made another application, this time for a 2 hectare (5 acre) site on the south shore of the lake. The proposal included a full-scale tourist camp and a 30 hectare (74 acre) option for "future development." Although the park was in agreement with development taking place in Yoho to ensure that visitors had places to go and stay, it was not excited about the prospect of full-scale development of the kind that had grown up around the Chateau at Lake Louise. Perhaps because the lingering spectre of Niagara Falls was still haunting park managers, the department issued a lease for 2 hectares (5 acres) but refused to approve a larger lease until a detailed proposal for the project was approved by senior bureaucrats and politicians in Ottawa. Clearly, the intention of the CPR was to develop a fine hotel at the lake and to use leasehold expansion to prevent other potential developers from building in the area. The park superintendent agreed that the lakeshore was an ideal location for a hotel but wanted to follow due process. Russell took no further steps toward expansion of the leasehold area but on August 1, 1923, approved a 21-year lease at $10 a year on the 2 hectare (5 acre) property at the edge of the lake. Although additional cabins were built at Lake O'Hara, approved construction of the lodge was delayed. Rather than building a lodge at Lake O'Hara, the railway diverted its resources to the construction of Wapta Lodge, at the summit of Kicking Horse Pass, which was to open at the same time the road from Lake Louise to Field was to be completed in the summer of 1925. The opening of the highway was delayed for two years, however, by which time the new lodge at Lake O'Hara would be finished too.

While work advanced on the Wapta camp, the trail was widened from the tracks at Hector to permit easier movement of building materials to the lake. Because of the proposed size of the lodge, it was not possible to use local forests to supply the timber for the project without completely altering the scenery around the building. To protect the integrity of the lodge view, the railway undertook the expense of shipping logs from Vancouver by rail to Hector. During the winter of 1925–26, lumber and other building supplies were hauled by wagon and then horse-drawn sleigh from the rail line to the lake. The foreman in charge of construction had two teams of horses working the track each day. On June 30, 1926, the $15,000 Lake O'Hara Lodge was officially opened. The lodge and the four older log cabins that had been moved around it could accommodate about 80 guests. As soon as the lodge opened, it became a popular destination for aficionados of mountain landscapes from all over the world. Visitors started booking their next year's visit as soon as they came. Lake O'Hara Lodge was not just a place to stay; it immediately became one of those exclusive places where sophisticated people gathered to appreciate place.

In 1929, the question arose in official park circles as to whether the CPR cabins at the lake were unlawfully erected within the legal 30.5 metre reservation along the edge of the water course. Although the details were not recorded, the debate over this issue was likely fairly hot, one side claiming that the railway had too many liberties inside the park, the other side arguing that the cabins had already been on site for years, so why was there a problem now? The proposal that the eight cabins be removed from the lakeshore was not acted upon. In 1931, the Alpine Club of Canada took possession of the old buildings on the original 2 hectare (5 acre) site in the meadows between the lake and McArthur Pass. The largest of these buildings was named Elizabeth Parker in honor of the remarkable Winnipeg woman who argued with a frustrated A. O. Wheeler that it would be an insult for Canada's national mountaineering body to simply be a wing of the American Alpine Club. She successfully lobbied for a separate club in Canada and then became secretary of the Alpine Club of Canada when it was formed in 1906.

Throughout the early 1930s further renovation of Lake O'Hara Lodge was undertaken to provide additional office space, a larger dining room, and new bathroom facilities. By 1944, when the lease for the property was renewed, the value of the lodge and surrounding facilities was pegged at $50,000. In 1951 a major kitchen facility and staff dining room were added to the building. By this time, the railway was arguing that the use of packhorses to supply the lodge was no longer adequate for its size or for the level of service it wanted to provide its guests. The railway requested that the road from Kicking Horse Pass be upgraded to allow trucks to carry supplies to the lodge. Although the decision was to change the ambiance of the O'Hara area for good, the department agreed to limited truck use. But the first era of tourism in O'Hara was also ending for another reason. In 1954 the Canadian Pacific Railway decided to sell its mountain chalet holdings, including those at Emerald Lake, Takakkaw Falls, Twin Falls, and Lake O'Hara. The new owners of Lake O'Hara Lodge were Claude Brewster and Austin Ford.

Change Comes to the Lodge

By 1958, the Brewster-Ford partnership was amended and the properties they held split between the two partners. Austin Ford became the sole owner of Lake O'Hara Lodge. As the popularity of the automobile increased and roads were extended all over the mountain national parks, more visitors came for shorter periods of time. Thus, access to Lake O'Hara was improved, and visitors were carried into O'Hara by bus. Some of the established patrons of the lodge were furious. Lillian Gest, an accomplished mountaineer and explorer in her own right, expressed her indignation over the changes that were taking place at the lodge:

Those at O'Hara who have enjoyed the quiet mountain atmosphere and some solitude among the high peaks and passes hope that these "improvements" will not mean an influx of one-day tourists and souvenir stands. O'Hara was made for climbers and hikers. Let's keep it that way.

Through most of the first half of the 20th century, chalets like Lake O'Hara Lodge were known for their outstanding hospitality, even though they offered few amenities. You had to be a very special kind of person to want to operate a lodge like this. You had to love living in the mountains and be able to put up with all the inconveniences that are a part of mountain life. You had to like visitors, and you had to contribute to their getting the most out of their experience regardless of weather. Everyone who ever owned or managed the lodge put a personal stamp on it. The people who lived and worked at Lake O'Hara Lodge often became legends in their own right. Lillian Gest, in her small but cherished, privately published History of Lake O'Hara, tells of one of these legends:

When the Canadian Pacific Railway first established the camp at Lake O'Hara in 1920–21, Mrs. Bill Brewster became the manager. It is said that the first guest was an Italian Prince. All the equipment of course had to be packed up on horses from Wapta Lake at Hector. The trail was very narrow; so narrow it was also said that a rider had to keep his toes turned in so as not to hit the trees and that it took "forever" to get up to the cabin with two crates of eggs. Bears were a great nuisance but the guests loved seeing them around — just as they do today! There were always strange mishaps occurring, such as the time when the pillows arrived but no mattresses. After Mrs. Brewster had turned pillows into mattresses, she learned that the camp at Yoho had all the mattresses but no pillows. Cooking was done in the small cabin and the facilities were meagre and primitive. Miss Sylvia Brewster, always known as "Sid", ran the Lodge the second year and continued to do so after it was moved to the lake.

In 1930 she married Sidney Graves who repaired both cabins and enlarged the newer one in the meadow during the years 1932–34; he also built trails and bridges for the CPR and was in charge of the horses at Wapta. He died tragically in 1945. Mrs. Graves carried on at the Lodge creating a friendly mountain atmosphere there which endeared her to many of her guests. The square dances she organized in which guests and staff joined were a feature of Saturday evenings. Mrs. Graves died in 1953 having stayed at Lake O'Hara seriously ill until three days before her death. She had been at O'Hara every summer for 33 years with the exception of the war years, 1942–45, when it was closed to guests

Trail Builders

Changes in access to Lake O'Hara only broadened the area's appeal. More and more people were coming every year, and trail systems were not up to the use they were receiving. Often to the consternation of local park officials, some of the lodge's regular visitors decided to take matters into hand and commit themselves to improving the trails around the lake and to surrounding beauty spots like Lake Oesa, Lake McArthur, and the Odaray and Opabin plateaus. The first of these was Dr. George K. K. Link, a professor of botany at the University of Chicago.

During the arid years of the later part of the 1920s, forest fires were increasingly an aspect of mountain life in the Pacific Northwest. In the summer of 1928, George "Tommy" Link and his wife, Adeline, had returned to their favourite holiday spot at Kintla Lake in Glacier National Park in Montana. Since the views in this part of the Rockies were almost completely obliterated by smoke, the Links decided to head north into Canada. On their first visit to Lake O'Hara, they were brought completely under its spell. Although there are differing accounts about this, they appear to have returned every summer for at least the next 14 years. During their earliest visits, George and Adeline worked their way deeply into local culture through close association with James Edward Hervey MacDonald and his friends Pete and Catharine Whyte of Banff.

Link's ambition in building new trails at O'Hara was to help visitors derive the greatest pleasure from intimate contact with the forests, meadows, and high, rocky promontories that make the area so special.

Link and his wife also wanted to ensure that while visiting these special places pilgrims did not destroy the very qualities they came to enjoy. The trails they developed were placed discreetly on the land. There was Royal Stag Meadow, a place where George and Adeline had encountered a huge elk. They also named places after people who had a demonstrable love for the O'Hara area. They named meadows for John Singer Sargent and J. E. H. MacDonald. Later a meadow was named for Glen Brook, then chief park warden in Yoho. The Links were becoming intimate with the country. As a result of their visits to favourite rocks and viewpoints, trails were developed to places like the Odaray Plateau. At first the trails were indicated only with rag streamers tied to branches. As the routes became better defined, they were marked by tree blazes, and then, in their final stages, rocks and fallen trees were removed to formalize the way.

In the summer of 1932 the Links were joined in their trail-building pursuits by Carson Simpson. Simpson was a prominent Philadelphia lawyer whose interests extended beyond the wonders of Lake O'Hara to Sherlock Holmes and all the mysteries of crime. Besides helping the Links with the trails and the evolving map of the area, Simpson enlisted the Links and other lodge guests to recreate photographs of an alleged meeting between Sherlock Holmes and Professor Moriarty on a Swiss glacier that looked surprisingly like the Opabin Glacier below Opabin Pass. While they were clearly having a lot of fun, the Links and Carson Simpson were also serious about the trails that radiated outward from the lodge. The LinkCarson map was beginning to complete itself, delicately civilizing the O'Hara wilderness with elegant paths and walkways that seemed to dissolve right into the rock work of the peaks.

Gasoline rationing and patriotic commitment to World War II decreed that Lake O'Hara Lodge be officially closed to guests between 1942 and 1945. Swiss guide Walter Feuz and his son Ronnie were retained as caretakers. Slim Rusch was retained to occasionally truck supplies into the lodge and to spell off the Feuzes when the bush began to wear away at them. George Link did not want the war to stand in the way of his love of Lake O'Hara. Somehow he managed to receive permission to return to the lake in the summers of 1942 and 1943, and he, Simpson, and Adeline put themselves up in the staff house behind the main lodge. In the summer of 1943, they built a trail on the north side of the lake, which was christened in late August when Adeline became the first person to make a complete circuit of Lake O'Hara on the new path. To commemorate the event, Walter Feuz carved a register in a tree near the outlet of the lake. It read: "1943 Trail Crew — G. K. K. Link, W. Feuz, Ronnie Feuz — Chef de Cuisine Mrs. A. D. Link, The Wiwaxy Trail." The core of the group later known as the Lake O'Hara Trails Club was now formed.

In September of 1943, the Links returned to Chicago with their hearts full of the glories of Lake O'Hara. But their joy was short-lived. Adeline suffered a stroke, and on November 20 she died. George Link was devastated. On August 1, 1944, Link and Carson Simpson strewed Adeline's ashes over her favourite rock on the Odaray Plateau. For the rest of the summer, Simpson and Link worked on the Wiwaxy Trail, where the idea to name the trail for Adeline presented itself. In the summer of 1945, the trail around Lake O'Hara was renamed the Adeline DeSale Link Trail.

On August 1, 1946, Link walked alone from Hector to Lake O'Hara to carry out a commemorative service for his wife on the shore of the lake. At the first rise on the trail, the botanist in Link was distracted by a profusion of wildflowers he could not help but visit. He re-emerged on the trail at a point where he could first see Mt. Odaray. It was while looking at Mt. Odaray that Link encountered a vision of his departed wife:

There it stood in full sunshine, snow blanketing its peak and the site of our rock! Suddenly it seemed as though Adeline stood on the trail waiting for me. She smiled, kissed me, and said, "Aren't we fortunate to be here together!" Her figure and face were those of the days when I courted her 30 years ago. She wore the same white waist and skirt, the same yellow tie she wore in those glo-

rious days. For an instant the image of her paralyzed face returned, but, strangely and wondrously, the sight of it no longer tore me to pieces. Instead, I greeted it. Some deepseated change had occurred within me.... And with that her lovely face reappeared with "the marvellous ray that used to light her eye. She became radiant and glorious and seemed suffused with blessedness. The experience filled me with warmth and with a feeling of peace and happiness. There flashed into my mind the thought, "You have experienced the naturalistic basis of the concepts, transfiguration, glorification, and beatification." I said to myself, "You are not merely Tommy Link walking to our beloved O'Hara; you are a pilgrim on a pilgrimage to a shrine." Shortly I also became aware that for the first time in almost three years I was humming aloud joyously. It was the Hymn of Thanksgiving and Praise after the storm in Beethoven's Pastoral Symphony.

If Tommy Link had been dedicated to the O'Hara ways and trails before, his enthusiasm for the wonders of Yoho were nothing compared to what they were now. O'Hara became solace for the grief Link suffered after the death of Adeline. His passion for the O'Hara area would be rivalled only by that of an Italian mountaineer, miner, and rock gardener.

Lorenzo Grassi: Mountaineer and Trail Maker

Lorenzo Grassi was born in the village of Falmenta in the mountainous province of Piedmont in Italy on December 20, 1890. In his adolescence, he became a woodsman, working with his father cutting trees in the forests near Grenoble, France. At the age of 20 Lawrence emigrated to Canada, where he worked as a section hand for the Canadian Pacific Railway near Thunder Bay. In 1913, he allowed the railway to bring him west to the Rockies, where he worked on the rugged Hector section of Yoho National Park. In the high and stony silence of the Great Divide, Grassi found his home.

In September of 1916, Grassi left the railway to become a miner in Canmore. Although he spent 30 years underground, Grassi never for a moment abandoned his great enthusiasm for the peaks. It was not long before Lawrence was recognized as an accomplished mountaineer. Small but powerful, Grassi made some important first ascents in the Rockies. Although it is not formally acknowledged, Grassi made the first solo ascent of Mt. Assiniboine, a feat accomplished in the summer of 1925. Grassi and another Canmore miner were the first to climb the east face of Cascade Mountain, up the almost-vertical wall that rises above the waterfall. In August of 1926, Grassi and another miner also claimed the first ascent of the impressive Eisenhower tower on Castle Mountain, an ascent that brought Grassi's abilities to the attention of the Alpine Club of Canada. Club members eagerly sought Grassi's leadership when they

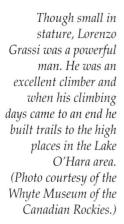

Though small in stature, Lorenzo Grassi was a powerful man. He was an excellent climber and when his climbing days came to an end he built trails to the high places in the Lake O'Hara area. (Photo courtesy of the Whyte Museum of the Canadian Rockies.)

wanted to climb renowned Mt. Louis near Banff, long recognized as one of the classic difficult rock climbs in North America. Grassi made more ascents of this mountain than any man of his time. In 1936, Lawrence was invited to join a highly touted combined Canadian and American expedition that hoped to make the first ascent of remote Mt. Waddington, the highest of the Coast Range peaks. Although bad weather prevented their success, Grassi's name became something of a household word in mountaineering circles.

Lawrence Grassi loved to climb, but he also loved to make trails. As early as 1924, when a labour strike closed the mine for weeks, Grassi spent the summer building trails from his backyard to the lakes and viewpoints above Canmore. A man of nearly superhuman strength, Grassi usually worked alone building trail after trail in what is now the Kananaskis, in Banff, and at Skoki near Lake Louise. But the most famous of all his trail work was done in Yoho. Tommy and Lawrence, Jon Whyte's definitive book on the ways and the trails of Lake O'Hara, The Lake O'Hara Trails Club, 1983, includes a story celebrating the small Italian's great strength. Jon Whyte credits the story to Don Harbridge.

The Canadian Parks Service still builds trails in Yoho to the high standards established by Tommy Link and Lorenzo Grassi. The trails of the O'Hara area look like they were placed naturally on the land.

Don's companions were John Hutchinson and Ted Asseltine. This is how Jon Whyte retold the story:

> *In June 1949 three teenagers camped near the Elizabeth Park Hut in Contentment Meadows. Damp clothes and small stoves had frustrated their pleasures a mite, and so they sought surcease from the clammy effects of the muck coming up from Wapta. They found in the bush a brute of an iron stove, but it was a quarter-mile or so from their camp. Two hours struggle with it,*

and the three boys managed to heave, haul, push, and shove it about half the distance. Then, having "other ambitions for the day than moving a very heavy cast iron stove ....we hurried to make lunch and get climbing." Twenty minutes later they looked up and beheld Lawrence Grassi carrying the stove toward them. "Where do you want it boys?" he asked, while the three of them stood dumbfounded.

Grassi became the area's first park warden in the summer of 1956. Although much of the early trail work at O'Hara had been done by Tommy Link and Carson Simpson, who had created the Lake O'Hara Trails Club in 1949, new paths up the steep walls and through the broken rock to Lake Oesa and Lake McArthur demanded more engineering ability than the club's ambitious volunteer founders possessed. Grassi's fine trails give one an appreciation for the ledge from which it is possible to safely experience the grandeur of the steep mountain views that make O'Hara so spectacular. Grassi's epic commitment to making all of the O'Hara region accessible to visitors is commemorated on the Oesa trail. Others too acknowledged the spirit and the generosity of this humble man. The famous parliamentarian J. S. Woodsworth met Grassi in 1937. "The world needs Grassis," he told the House of Commons in 1938. "In the realm of the spirit, in the search after truth, in the field of social relationships, in international affairs, we need trail makers — men who will seek new paths, make the rough places smooth, bridge the chasms that now prevent human progress, point the way to higher levels and loftier achievements."

Retiring from trail building a few months short of his 75th birthday, Lawrence Grassi lived out his remaining days in Canmore, just east of Banff. In the end, just as in the beginning, Grassi continued to have a profound impact on everyone he met. After Grassi died in 1980, twin lakes above Canmore were renamed for him. Also in honor of his generosity, courage, and mountain spirit, one of Canmore's schools was named for him.

In 1975, the Fords sold Lake O'Hara Lodge to Michael and Marsha Laub and friends. Shortly after, Tim Wake, who had worked for the Fords at Lake O'Hara, also became one of the Lodge's managing partners. Later, Tim's wife, Leslee, became a partner as well. Despite changes in tourist expectations, huge increases in visitation, and the radically altered status of wilderness in Canada, the lodge and the lake have retained their dignity and character. Although it is hard to believe, limits to access, improved trails, and a better understanding of the carrying capacity of the area have actually improved the Lake O'Hara experience. As the legend of the lake demands special considerations from everyone who visits it, a reverence for the wonder of O'Hara is prefigured in every visit there. Because people have to plan to go there and because the fragility of the area demands that visitors be careful to stay on trails and to minimize their every impact on the sensitive spirit of place that makes it special, O'Hara has remained a living shrine for those who most appreciate the Rockies. Jon Whyte summed it up near the end of his book on Lake O'Hara when he said: "The trail has no end, 'the road leads ever on,' the path leads back to the garden, the fount of inspiration, the source of the soul. Lake O'Hara, once a garden, became a garden. Eden becomes paradise."

Martin Sam (left) was a native Kootenay and Joe Eugene (right) was a native Shuswap. They pair started working on the trail crew in Kootenay National Park in 1946 and came to Yoho in 1955. Together they built and maintained much of Yoho's trail system. (Photograph by Glen Brook.)

When the Canadian Pacific built Mt. Stephen House, Yoho was still very much a remote wilderness. (Photograph courtesy of the Canadian Parks Service.)

Chapter 6

Field: The Capital City of Wonder

On November 25, 1885, Canada's first national reserve was set aside by an Order-In-Council in Ottawa. This reserve legally protected a small area of land around Banff's Sulphur Mountain hot springs. The following year, the government announced the establishment of three other park reserves in accordance with its developing policy to protect prime mountain scenery and resources from exploitation in the wake of the completion of the Canadian Pacific Railway. The three new areas included, 78 square kilometres (30 square miles) in the Selkirks, which now form the basis of Glacier National Park, 26 square kilometres (10 square miles) around Griffen Lake in Eagle Pass west of Revelstoke, and 26 square kilometres (10 square miles) encompassing Mt. Stephen near the town of Field.

Since British Columbia was a full-fledged province and Alberta was still part of a developing North West Territories, there was some difference in the way national parks were established in each place. When British Columbia entered Confederation, it did so with the proviso that all of the public lands within its borders would be retained by the province except for a tract of land 32 kilometres wide on either side of the Canadian Pacific Railway. It was within this railway belt that the province's national parks would be set aside. As part of a territory, however, Alberta did not gain complete control over its natural resources until 1930, a fact that had a great impact on the location and size of its national parks. This difference in jurisdictional powers between Alberta and British Columbia gave rise to radically differing opinions about how the resources in these new parks were to be managed. The province of British Columbia maintained that although national parks were a good thing, they should not interfere with the orderly and appropriate exploitation of the natural resources of the province. Thus, it came to be that fish and game regulations and mining and forest management were undertaken differently in British Columbia's national parks than they were in the parks on the other side of the Great Divide in Alberta.

Creating a National Park

The idea of national reserves was still in a fragile infancy in Canada at the time Yoho was born, as shown by a scheme concocted by surveyor Otto Klotz after his initial explorations of the upper reaches of the Kicking Horse Valley. Observing how the entire Kicking Horse River was constricted through the Natural Bridge, Klotz believed that it was simply "a question of time" before a dam was built across the valley. Klotz argued that the dam would be relatively inexpensive given the nature of the terrain and that it would change the unsightly gravel flat on which Field was built into a lake, "creating a scene beautiful amidst the sublime." Even J. J. McArthur agreed with the plan. If there had not been mining potential in the valley, the idea might have come to fruition. Thus, the park was saved when one extraction industry cancelled out another.

In June of 1889, another Dominion land surveyor, W. S. Drewry, began his explorations of the main ranges of the Canadian Rockies. His reports to Ottawa included enthusiastic descriptions of the mining and smelting potential of every mountain area he visited. Drewry, in the footsteps of James Hector, reported favourably on the timber potential of the Kicking Horse Valley. He also commented on the mining potential of the valley already noted by Tom Wilson as early as 1884. Both logging and mining would later become major issues in Yoho National Park.

Perhaps because the resource base of the valley had barely been explored, the reserve area established at the base of Mt. Stephen seemed a natural place to

A squatter's shanty in Field prior to the development of the town plan that laid the community out in a grid. (Courtesy of the Canadian Parks Service.)

create a park. It was well placed along main divisional points along the railway, it was at the base of the maintenance challenge of the Big Hill on Kicking Horse Pass, it was a convenient place for weary travellers to break their journey, and as Tom Wilson had indicated as early as 1882, it was a good place to graze horses. The special status of the this canyonlike site was confirmed when Mt. Stephen House was built in Field in the summer of 1886. In the autumn of 1888, the Canadian Pacific Railway applied to the federal government to purchase all the land adjacent to Mt. Stephen House and the nearby railway station at the centre of Field. It appears that the success of Mt. Stephen House had attracted undesirables to the area and the CPR wanted to remove them or, at the least, remove themselves from the problem. Here is how the railway explained it:

Objectionable persons of both sexes had squatted upon lands near the Depot. The Company desired the control asked for so that these squatters could be summarily removed and so that others of like character could be prevented by the Company's officers from taking up their residence at this point.

It seems that right from the start, Field was bound to attract more than its share of transients and squatters. A post office was opened in the General Store in Field in 1889 to serve locals and squatters alike. The first post master was H. G. Parson. Although it was moved several times over the years, since 1960 the post office has been located on Kicking Horse Avenue, next to the police station. Records indicate that J. G. Hands became the first teacher in Field in 1895 though others may have taught less formally in an ad hoc school operated around town. By all accounts from the time, Field was turning into a shanty town. Although the government was sympathetic to the railway's problems, it had other agendas and didn't grant exclusive rights to the land. The problem grew worse until 1898, when an exasperated Charles Drinkwater, formerly private secretary to Prime Minister John A. Macdonald and now assistant to the president of Canadian Pacific Railway, wrote the Minister of the Interior with a further plea for a monopoly on the land in Field. Drinkwater's plea was eloquent and did change the government's position on the matter:

The establishment of Field as a divisional point and the consequent enlargement of our premises there have evidently induced squatters to take possession of sites on which buildings will be erected and in which liquor will be sold. It is very necessary in order to secure the safe operation of the line between Field and Golden where as you know there are very heavy grades requiring the most careful handling of trains that no places where liquor can be sold to our men should be established near our works. ... We should probably be in a better position than the Government to deal with undesirable squatters if we had title to the lands....

This photograph was taken by William Notman and Son's in 1887. The view is from the steps of Mt. Stephen House in Field. The town wasn't composed of much more than a few shacks and a lot of tree trunks. The Van Horne Range is in the distance.

So with a little bit of ink and a piece of paper, Drinkwater got rid of all the prostitutes and bootleggers in Field. Although the railway was not permitted to actually gain title to the land, Section 17, Township 28, Range 18 West of the 5th Meridian adjacent to Mt. Stephen House, was surveyed into lots and leased to the railway and other favoured parties. The town of Field was born with only one proviso. To protect the railway's interests, the leases could be cancelled immediately if liquor were to be sold by the owners of the lease. Dominion land surveyor A. P. Patrick devised a town lot system in the summer of 1903. This survey, however, did not satisfy the Surveyor General and necessitated another attempt at laying out the town. This survey, conducted by J. E. Ross in the summer of 1904, developed the grid on which the town of Field is still laid out today. With the survey completed, the leases let, and the surrounding area protected by law as Mt. Stephen Reserve, the railway could at last rid itself of the squatter problem. With the hotel as the central attraction of the park, Field began to develop a genteel reputation among the more sophisticated clientele the railway catered to during those early, golden days of mountain tourism. These idyllic days, as Arthur Oliver Wheeler alluded to in 1905, did not last for long:

J confess to a preference for the good old days when time was not so valuable, and remember one morning in Field, when the boast of the CPR that its conductors were endowed with true Parisian politeness, was fully exemplified. I had been eating my breakfast slowly and looking round at the wonderful fluffy things (pussy willows) and other bric-a-brac with which the centre table was loaded, when the conductor came in, hat in hand, and remarked, 'The train is waiting, sir! As soon as you have finished we will start.' Now it's, 'All aboar-r-r-d.'

If Wheeler were alive today, he might not speak so highly of the politeness of the Parisians. Nor would he attest to consistently high levels of service excellence in the Rockies. He might, however, agree that the great success of Van Horne's railway hotels brought immediate changes to the structures themselves, to the communities that surrounded them, and to the national parks in which they were situated.

The growth of railway tourism presented some very large contradictions for the first park managers, who were charged with making some sort of long-

The "Big Hill" above Field necessitated constant maintenance requiring a lot of manual labour. A thriving community grew up around the needs of the railway. At the turn of the century, when this photograph was taken, Field probably boasted a population of more than 400.

119

term sense out of the rapid change that was affecting the West. At first, the wilderness character of the mountain West was seen as an advantage. In February of 1901, Charles Drinkwater wrote again to the Minister of the Interior suggesting that the spectacular waterfalls and the great glaciers in the Yoho Valley north of Field be set aside as a mountain park. Drinkwater also offered that the CPR was poised to make extensive improvements to its hotel and to build new stables, corrals, trails, and bridges to capitalize on the growing tourism potential of Yoho. Using this opportunity to apply for the use of more land, Drinkwater made bid for a 9 hectare (22.7 acre) lease across from the Field station for the purposes of beginning work on the stables and corrals. Deputy Minister James Smart was all for the idea of the park but was unsure what the legal ramifications of an application to the province of British Columbia might yield. It appears that the 1888 Order-In-Council that created the Mt. Stephen reserve overlooked the fact that the new parks it created at Glacier, Eagle Pass, and Mt. Stephen were within the railway belt and therefore outside the jurisdiction of the Dominion Lands Act. It was at this juncture in the history of Yoho that provincial laws relating to distribution and drinking of liquor and to hunting and fishing and mining and timber rights were seen to have jurisdiction over Dominion park regulations. Once this was recognized, the establishment of the park went forward with the only major argument being about its name. Names suggested for the new park included Field Reserve Park, and Wapta Falls Park. The latter name was confusing to locals since they commonly held Wapta Falls to be the falls on the Kicking Horse near its junction with the Beaverfoot River. As it turned out, a party of American tourists had attempted to change the name of Takakkaw Falls to Wapta Falls. This having failed, Van Horne's choice of Native names for the Yoho Valley and Takakkaw Falls prevailed. On December 14, 1901, the 2138 square kilometre (825.5 square mile) Yoho Park Reserve was created by an Order-In-Council in Ottawa. As the order read, one of the principal reasons for the park's creation was that it was of no use for human settlement:

> ... *It is hereby ordered with reference to the tract of land which is near Field on the line of the Canadian Pacific Railway and the boundaries which are shown in red upon the accompanying tracing and being part of the lands in the Province of British Columbia to which the provisions of Chapter 56 of the Revised Statutes of Canada relate, that, as such tract of land is not suitable for ordinary settlement, but because of the glaciers, large waterfalls, and other wonderful and beautiful scenery within its boundaries it is adapted for the purposes of a Public Park....*

As soon as the park was created, critics, including Drinkwater, claimed that it was already too large. A powerful lobby had already been established to have the valuable timber on the east slope of the Beaverfoot Valley excluded from the

Mt. Stephen House was not the only hotel in Field. Though the Strand Hotel was small, it is remembered by many who lived in it before they could find more permanent accommodation in town.

park. Although some of the most interesting forests in all of Yoho were in this area, the lobbyists for logging argued successfully that there were "no special scenic attractions in that neighbourhood which we need to preserve." The great cedars and Douglas fir trees that James Hector described in his journals were never seen by tourists. In 1907, the park was reduced by 272 square kilometres (105 square miles). It was reduced again in 1911 to 1310 square kilometres (506 square miles). Area neutral land swaps continued until 1930, when the park's boundaries were frozen by law and the area of the park increased to about 1313 square kilometres (507 square miles), the size it remains today.

As the railway brought more and more tourists, however, the undeveloped state of the Rockies posed a problem for visitors illequipped for adventure. Yoho was initially administered by the superintendent of Rocky Mountains Park, whose office was in Banff. In 1905, Superintendent Howard Douglas reported on the lamentable lack of facilities in Yoho:

> At the time when this tract came under jurisdiction there were absolute-
> ly no improvements upon it except the line of the Canadian Pacific
> Railway.....Owing to the lack even of bridal paths, travelling was very diffi-
> cult, and only a few venturesome persons had the hardihood to brave the risks

of exploring this unknown country. The beauties of the Yoho Valley had been spoken of at rare intervals, but there was little tangible knowledge of the configuration of the country or its possibilities as a point of interest for the tourist.

As the railway continued to bombard the rest of the civilized world with advertising, the relative obscurity of Yoho Park vanished. In 1902, Tom Wilson had signed a contract with the railway for livery and outfitting operations in Field and Laggan. Wilson's new partner in the deal, Bob Campbell, became responsible for services provided to rail passengers at Field and Emerald Lake. As Wilson was tying up the outfitting operations in Yoho, St. Andrew's Presbyterian Church was moved from the vanishing town of Donald to Field and renamed St. Stephen's. The same year, Emerald Lake Chalet was opened. Two years later, a wagon road was completed to Emerald Lake. Traces of this "tally-ho road" can still be easily seen across from the present town of Field. By 1905, Yoho could boast its own park superintendent, O. D. Hoar, and a handsome new administration building in Field.

Fixing Up Field

By this time, the unsightly condition of the town was becoming a government concern. Although Field had been surveyed the year before, leases had not been let to alleviate the squatter problem or to allow for further development that would enable the squalor of shacks to be replaced with more permanent buildings. After a brief visit to Field, Deputy Minister of the Interior T. G. Rothwell was appointed commissioner of an inquiry respecting land and lease claims in the town. Rothwell emphasized what the locals already clearly understood. The town needed some effective organization to prevent it from going the way of so many towns in the west that had become impossible to live in because of a lack of applied planning. Rothwell understood the potential position of the town as the headquarters of one of Canada's most important national parks:

The situation from the scenic point of view is fine, but unless the Company or the Dominion assumes charge of and makes all necessary improvements including the grading of streets, the laying down of sidewalks, the establishment of a water service for fire protection and for domestic use, and most material of all, the providing of proper drainage, this little townsite ...will become a plague spot and an eye sore to the Company's beautiful hotel and its depot, and other buildings upon the Company's lands at this point – and it should not be forgotten that Field is not only named but is, because of its situation, the "Gateway" to the Yoho Valley with its magnificent natural beauties.

Rothwell also went on to compare Field with Banff, something that hasn't likely been done since: …"if Field is to be dealt with as Banff is and is to be made what it should be, [it will become] one of the beautiful spots in one of the most beautiful national parks in the world."

In 1906, the park's first game warden, Roxy Hamilton, took up employment in the park. In 1907, after Rothwell's report had been submitted to the Minister of the Interior, Superintendent Hoar met with the railway and the townspeople to arrive at estimated costs for the relocation of the streets in Field and for the renovation of the town's more permanent buildings. During the winter of 1907–08, Bob Campbell's saddle horse concession lease with the railway in Field and Laggan expired. The operation was taken over in the summer of 1908 by the Brewster brothers of Banff. To offset the cost of this acquisition, Brewster applied to the railway for a revised livery tariff that saw the price of a single rig trip from Field to Emerald Lake jump to three dollars, which was also what Brewster charged for a return trip from Field to Ottertail for up to three people.

In 1909, O. D. Hoar was replaced by George E. Hunter, who became the superintendent of both Yoho and Glacier national parks. In that same year the Spiral Tunnels were completed on the Big Hill, eliminating the deathdefying rail descent from the summit of Kicking Horse Pass into Field. Associated with the new tunnels was the construction of a new roundhouse with two stalls in Field. In the winter of 1909, the project of relocating and rebuilding the town around the parameters set by the 1904 Ross survey was hastened by an avalanche that slid off the shoulder of Mt. Burgess, destroying many of the buildings that had been constructed on the north side of the Kicking Horse River. The avalanche was of such force that the winds emanating from it shattered windows on the north side of Mt. Stephen House. As the town gradually rearranged itself along the new grid system, park leases were formalized at a standard 42 years, with the annual rent fixed at $8.00 a year for inside lots and $9.50 for corner lots. Settlement of the leasing issue allowed for the amalgamation of both CPR and federal communities in Field into a single unified town. The population of Field at this time was likely no more than 500 people.

By May 1910, First Avenue, Kicking Horse Avenue, First Street, and Centre street were cleared and graded and a number of new homes constructed. Civic-minded inhabitants initiated a town beautification program. Balm of Gilead, a sterile hybrid variety of the common cottonwood poplar tree, was planted along the new roads, along the railway tracks, and in the occasional backyard. Some of these trees are now huge and offer plenty of shade in summer. In 1912, the Ottertail Drive was completed west of Field, and the town could now boast the longest and highest carriage bridge in the Rockies. In 1912, Field residents were wowed by a royal visit by the Duke and Duchess of Connaught and Princess Patricia, who visited the Natural Bridge and Emerald Lake. Although Field continued to change gradually during the next decade, the World War I decreased tourism in the area. In 1918, when the war ended, the railway converted Mt. Stephen House into a combined YMCA and railroad bunkhouse. Superintendent Russell was not pleased with the decision. He believed it had been made in too great a hurry without due consideration of its impact on tourism and the town. This account is from records Russell left behind in the park:

Mt. Stephen Hotel, which up to this year has been run as a first-class hotel under the able management of the Canadian Pacific Railway Company was recently turned over to the management of the railway workers, who completely occupy this large building. This left us almost without accommodation for the travelling public in Field and made it necessary for all persons wishing to stop off to drive out either to the Emerald Lake Chalet or to the Yoho Camp immediately upon arrival, and as the accommodation at both of these places was fairly limited, many were disappointed who wished to stay over.

Although it was still very much the centre of the town and the park, the hotel's days as a centrepiece of railway tourism promotion came to an end.

Daily Life in Field

Details of when buildings are constructed and when they begin their decline are significant historical facts, especially in a small town like Field, but they do not say much about what it was like to live in a place like Yoho in the early days of tourism. To sense the ambiance of the times, we must rely on the accounts of those who were present then. Gerry Andrews worked as a waiter in the YMCA at Mt. Stephen House in the summer of 1919. His lucid and remarkably well written but unpublished account of that summer gives us some insight into what Field and Yoho were like after the Great War.

The "Y" at Field, in 1919, was housed in Mount Stephen House, the old CPR hotel, built in the late 1880's. It was an enormous wooden gingerbread structure, fronting on the station platform. Its coffee shop, open all hours, catered mainly to railway crews, and to day-coach passengers who could get a quick, cheap snack there. Field was a Divisional Point where crews and locomotives from Calgary and Revelstoke were changed and coaches serviced. This took about half an hour. At that time and season there were at least six passenger trains each way each day. Highways were not yet built, so all through travel was by rail.

I reported to Mr. Rice, the "Y" Secretary, and was given a small bedroom, one floor up overlooking the station. I was put on night shift in the coffee shop — 10 pm to 8 am seven days a week, pay about $40 per month, "all found".

This was nearly twice what I got as a "Soldier of the Soil" in 1918. The seven-day week seemed hardly compatible with "Christian" in YMCA. I soon got into the routine, if a bit clumsy at first. I never became adept at carrying umpteen plates or cups with coffee with one arm.

A Chinese cook presided over the huge gloomy old kitchen behind. In quiet hours after midnight this area was in darkness except near the cook stove. At such times, to carry an overloaded tray of dishes to the sink, I momentarily switched on the lights. This revealed hordes of cockroaches galloping across the concrete floor to cover in dark corners — revolting!

Clientele for my shift were mostly freight crews, sometimes cranky, being away from their homes in Calgary or Revelstoke. I stood my ground against the bullies but discovered there were some "good guys" too. I contrived to eat some breakfast before going off duty and supper after going on at night — but without much appetite. Often I made a bag lunch to eat outdoors. The quiet hour was about 4 am when I could hardly keep my eyes open. But by 8 am I was very wide awake. Instead of going to bed I had to get out in the glorious sun and scenery. There were easy hikes to beautiful and interesting places. I felt hemmed in by the four nearby mountains, Stephen, Dennis, Burgess and Field, which cradled the town. The problem, aggravated by the noise of trains below my window, was to get enough sleep.

The thunder of eastbound freights grinding upgrade past the station was appalling. The routine was to assemble the train in the yards on a sizable flat west of town. The locomotives were oil-burning steam monsters, two in front to pull and one at the rear to push. When all was ready, the lead engines would go into reverse, just enough to close the slack in all couplings between the cars. When the pusher felt the impact it gave a short toot. The response was two toots from the front engine. then all would open full throttle ahead — with a cacophony of hissing steam in clouds and skidding drive wheels — a veritable tour de force. The lead engines would pass the station at about ten mph with the ground shaking under the tremendous load and power. When the pusher passed, the whole train would be on the upgrade and slowed down to walking speed. The battle of power versus gravity was gigantic and the noise deafening.

One day a friendly pusher engineer asked me if I would like a ride with him up through the Spiral Tunnels. He said I should be near the track about ten o'clock, out of sight just beyond the station. I was there and as he passed, I hopped on the step and climbed up into the cab. The fireman, not much older than I, sat on a leather cushion on the left with his hand on the fuel control — pretty soft! His pay would be more than twice mine. The engineer sat on the right, at the throttle. It was exciting to be carried along in the bosom of this dragon monster. In about half an hour we saw the beautiful Yoho Valley on our left and then entered the lower spiral tunnel. Lingering smoke from the front engines was suffocating and I fainted, partly from nervous tension. They revived me with a cold air jet and thought it a big joke. I survived the second tunnel. Then, at a siding near the summit, the lead engine and the pusher were detached, allowing the rest of the train to move on east. The two extra engines then hooked together and returned downgrade to Field, stopping in the yards past the station. I thanked my hosts for such a wonderful experience and walked back to the "Y" and to bed — to dream of space travel in a steam leviathan.

Andrews returned to Field to work again in the summer of 1921. He earned a university degree in 1930 and eventually went on the become the Surveyor General of British Columbia. Quite an achievement for a summer waiter at Mt. Stephen House in Field.

Young Norris Crump

But Gerry Andrews would not be the only one to use his Field experiences to advance his career. Some of the local boys made good, too. T. H. Crump came

Even after Mt. Stephen House became a railway YMCA, it remained the centre of town. Every activity seemed to centre around this graceful old hotel. (Photograph courtesy of the Canadian Parks Service.)

to Field to work as a brakeman on the Big Hill in 1891. He married Nell Edwards in 1895, and they had two children in Field before the family was transferred to Revelstoke. where a third child, Norris Roy Crump, was born in 1904. The family moved back to Field in 1906 when the senior Crump was promoted to trainmaster. In 1910 the family moved to Vancouver and then back to Revelstoke in 1915. By 1920, young Norris Roy had decided to follow in his father's footsteps and hitch his career to the railway star. He apprenticed in locomotive maintenance at the Field roundhouse between 1920 and 1922. His residence was the railroad YMCA. Donald Bain, a railroad historian from Calgary, likes to tell a story told to him by Archie Cameron about this period in Crump's life. Archie Cameron was an engineer who worked out of Field. One summer afternoon, in 1921 or 1922, Cameron went in to Crump's room to ask if he wanted to play baseball. When Crump declined because he was studying, Cameron asked if Crump was working toward being president. Many years later, Cameron wrote to Crump who lived in Montreal to tell him he was going to be visiting. Crump met him at Windsor Station and said, "I made it." When N. R. Crump said he had made it, he wasn't kidding. Crump had become the chairman of the CPR.

Field In The Early Twenties

Nowhere is the ambiance of early Field better characterized than in an account of the park offered by an itinerant young man named Ernie Les Plant, who rode the rails to Field in the summer of 1921. Thinking he might be able to find work as a farm laborer on the prairies, young Ernie hopped a freight train in Vancouver and, after a brief stop in Revelstoke, arrived in a small entourage of other hobos in Field. While the ragged party was hanging around in the General Store in Field, the local Mountie, Tom Corliss, inquired how they had got to town. After admitting that they had stolen a ride on an eastbound frieght, the Mountie invited them to step into his office across the street, where Ernie and his new friends were placed under arrest. Noting that the boys were starving, the Mountie then returned to the General Store for liver, onions, bread, butter, and potatoes and prepared a meal the young hoboes would gratefully remember for the rest of their lives.

Judgment came at 2:00 pm the same day. The judge, according to Les Plant, "read the riot act" to the young men and fined them each $5.00 and $4.50 in court costs. The other hoboes had the money to pay the fines. Les Plant did not and was sentenced to "thirty days in the pokey." Les Plant's account of what happened next says a great deal about what the town was like at that time:

> The jail was a small building, about 20 feet square, a small part at the front was the office. The jail had a table stove, some cooking pots and pans and

a sink, so it wasn't so bad. One cell in the corner had an upper and lower berth or bunk and this is where I was to sleep. The doors of the cage as well as the doors to the outside were never locked, because of fire, and because there was no guard or watchman. If someone was real bad, that means doing more than riding the rods, they would be put under lock and key, and would be put on the first train to Golden, where they had a proper jail.

The Mountie told me I could wander around town, and if I could pick up a job, I could maybe get enough money to pay my fine. But who would hire a kid out of jail? However, the Mountie told me that when it came meal time I was to go over to the railroad "Y" and go into the dining room and tell the girl I was from the jail and they would feed me, at no cost. I was told the police had to pay for my keep and that is why they wanted me to get a job or money to pay their fine.

The following Sunday afternoon, the Mountie came into the jail with a heavyset local man, named Ray Morrison, who inquired as to whether the young hobo had any logging experience. Les Plant answered that although he wasn't a logger, he could cut wood. The man left and the Mountie returned to tell young Ernie to go across the bridge over the Kicking Horse River to a small cabin occupied by a cowboy and to tell him "the Mountie sent you." The police-

One of the most interesting people to hang around in the Yoho Valley was cowboy song-writer and performer Wilf Carter. It is claimed that he wrote many of his most popular tunes in Field or at Emerald Lake Lodge. (Photograph courtesy of the Whyte Museum of the Canadian Rockies.)

man gave Les Plant a sweater, two blankets, a half pound of tobacco, some ciga-
rette papers, and a couple of magazines. He explained that he wanted the blankets back but that Les Plant could keep the rest.

After arriving on the other side of the river, Les Plant was informed that he
was now the leader of a pack train bound for the backcountry of the Yoho
Valley. A few hours later, the pack train arrived at the Summit Lake Tea Room
at the crest of Yoho Pass, where he again met Morrison, who informed him of
his new duties as camp cook for a trail crew building bridges in the Yoho Valley.
As the days passed, Les Plant gradually learned to cook. One afternoon, while
alone in camp, the young cook struck up a conversation with a lone hiker who
had stopped to say hello. As is customary on the trail, Les Plant offered the
hiker a meal. Only later, after the man was full of macaroni and cheese, did Les
Plant learn that the hiker was John Philip Sousa, the famous American band
leader. Les Plant's glorious sojourn in the Yoho Valley ended shortly afterwards,
when at last he learned the nature of his employer. Les Plant tells the story best:

*One day Ray took off for Field to get some supplies. He was gone for
about two days. He hiked in, but had a packhorse to come back on and another
with supplies. On his return, we could hear him singing miles away down the
Yoho Valley. That name, "The Beautiful Yoho Valley" was the name of one of
Wilf Carter's songs. (He was the singing cowboy at that time.) Ray arrived at
camp, drunk, and were the other two fellows glad to see him, because he had an
extra bottle. They had had a drink. Then the boss said to me, "I got your
cheque and cashed it and paid your fine, and bought two bottles so we could
celebrate. Here is your change, and thanks for the drinks." "Wait a minute, do
they pay prisoners to work?" "You haven't been a prisoner, you have been
working for the Parks of Canada …"*

The Italian Community

It was not just town planning and beautification programs that caused the
character of Field to change in the 1920s. The type of people who lived in the
community began to change also. With an influx of immigrant railway workers,
the community began to stabilize. The largest ethnic community to settle in
early Field was Italian. Much of what is remembered about the early days of the
Italian community in Field is owed to Mary Decicco Roberts, whose elegantly
written accounts of her family's life in Field were submitted to historian Pat
Rutherford at the time of Yoho's centennial in 1986. Mary Roberts recalled that
the first wave of Italian residents arrived in the very early days of the town,
between the turn of the century and the 1920s. The second wave arrived after
World War II, in the late 1940s and early 1950s. Most came to work on the railway, and they mostly settled in the western part of town. Gardening was a
large part of their recreational activity, and many took pride in their home

flower and vegetable gardens, often competing with other Italians in the community for the best sweet peas or asters. The Italians were also famous for the wines they made and freely shared with their neighbors at parties and after sporting events.

Of the 17 Italian families who came to work and live in Yoho, 15 were from the same region in Italy, the province of Cosenza in the south. After they moved to Field, they did not maintain an Italian society as such, probably because there were too few of them for any kind of structured group, but the Italian community did play an important role in the affairs of the town. The women were all involved in the work of St. Joseph's Catholic Church, though not many of the Italian men attended services with their families. In summer, the Catholics held a bazaar on the lawns of the YMCA. They would hang Japanese lanterns in and around their garden beds and would play games of chance during the bazaar's evening festivities.

Mary Decicco Roberts also reported that the Italians formed informal musi-

Part of the "Italian Community" out for a Sunday walk sometime in the mid-1920's or early 1930's. From left to right, Mrs. John Muzzillo, daughter Adelina, Mrs. Peter Decicco and Mrs. Sam Muzzillo. (Photo coutesy of Mary Decicco Roberts.)

cal groups. A few of the men played banjos or mandolins and kept the musical traditions of their homeland intact in Field. The greatest source of entertainment for the men was the bocce games on pleasant summer evenings in front of the Monarch Hotel. Bocce is the Italian equivalent to lawn bowling, played by two teams of two players each, and it was played out on the road. In an evening 8 or 10 men would take turns playing a series of games. The winning two-man team would be treated to beer after the game, and the kids would have a turn to play. If the men felt good about winning, the kids would get ice cream after their game.

Although the people in this community seldom saw themselves as adventurers, it surely took a great deal of courage to leave country, friends, and relatives to venture into the unknown in a place such as Canada. No doubt they were driven by a need to improve their lot in life. The southern part of Italy must have been difficult for young men and families who needed work, food and refuge. Mary Robert's mother, Marrietta Decicco, cried for 6 months steadily when she first arrived. Her husband, Peter Decicco, had no patience with some of the other members of the Italian community who complained about this new land. He would often remind them that many times in the old country they had gone hungry and that pocket money was unheard of there.

Italian families like the Deciccos, the Colonnas, the Arcaris, the Perris, and the Dimaulos helped make Field into a real town. The Italians provided a good life for their children. Roberts recalls that most grew up in comfortable homes with loving families and a loving community. The community provided the children with a good basic education and lots of simple entertainment. Best of all, she says, they were able to become good Canadians who came to love Canada as their own land without sacrificing their Italian roots and culture.

Mining

Although Field in the 1920s still was not a model of elegant living, it was a bustling place. Not only was it a centre of tourism, it was also a major railway divisional point. The town prospered to a large extent because of nearby mining and logging operations, which because of the province's early claim to the mineral rights along the railway belt, were conducted in and around the park.

Although the federal government had fought hard to make a case against resource extraction in its national reserves after it discovered the flaw in its original designation of the areas in 1886, the province of British Columbia continued to promote mining and logging as a way of stimulating its developing economy. A compromise on the matter had been reached in 1919 under the Banff-Windermere Roads Agreement, which created Kootenay National Park, but the status of existing mining and logging rights did not change until the National Parks Act was passed in 1930. By then, however, mining and logging claims were well established inside Yoho Park. Park officials and visitors alike simply had to put up with them until they expired or were terminated when the resources were exhausted. Even though much of the mining in the park was concentrated around Field or in the Ice River – Ottertail areas, it seemed for a time that it was difficult to go anywhere without running into miners in Yoho. The largest and most productive of the Yoho mines were the Monarch and Kicking Horse Mines, located at the head of the Kicking Horse Valley, just above Field.

In his few comments on the geology of the upper Kicking Horse Valley, James Hector mentioned "splintery iron shales" and "ferruginous [iron] beds" . Tom Wilson expanded substantially on Hector's observations by declaring potential mining opportunities below Mt. Stephen. Wilson's story about how he squandered the mining rights for Mt. Stephen is a classic in the I-just-missed-getting-rich-quick history of mining lore:

In the spring of 1884 I made a partnership with Jim Wright and with him went prospecting. Jim later became president of the Chamber of Mines at Smithers, B.C. We prospected the whole of that summer.

There was at Holt City at that time [near Castle Mountain] two broth-ers, George and Jim Kauffman. Jim ran a saloon and George was a prospector. They were great lads to argue and one day they held a long debate on the mer-its of hot water versus cold water as a whiskey chaser. Following the classic debate they were always known as "Hot-water Jimmy" and "Coldwater George". At that time the Public Works Act prohibited the sale of intoxicating liquors within ten miles of the construction work, but law was as efficient as any prohibition statute. Liquor was very hard to get only without money.

One day "Hot-water Jimmy" said he would like to have some mineral specimens to decorate the back of his bar, so the next time that I went to the foot of Mt. Stephen I gathered some for him. Directly "Cold-water George" saw the specimens he became very excited and asked what I intended doing with the find. I told him that I was letting it alone and showed him the assay-er's report.

"Show me where it is, turn it over to me and I will at least make a grub-stake out of it," he said.

I agreed and so the first time that Jim Wright and I went that way we located and staked the claim, then turned it over to "Cold-water" and he recorded it in Golden. He raised a grubstake, got a man named Hansen to go in with him, and did some work on it that summer.

An assayer named De Wolfe had settled at Golden and this man put an old country mining firm in touch with "Cold-water", "Hot-water" and Hansen, with the result that the three sold their claim that fall for $21,000. This was the claim that Jim Wright and I had made them a present of and that today is the big Monarch Mine near Field.

The public appearance of the first mineral claim by Tom Wilson and Jim Wright in 1884, and the completion of the main line of the railway the following year, set off a minor prospecting rush in Yoho. Within that single 1884 season, 135 mineral claims were staked in between Kicking Horse Pass and the Spillamacheen River. It was perhaps fortuitous that the dispute over who owned the mineral resources inside the railway belt in British Columbia slowed development of these claims, for many of them proved unproductive because of prohibitive transportation costs and the lack of smelting facilities nearby. Although Wilson had been smoked on the Monarch Mine deal, he continued prospecting in the Ottertail, Beaverfoot, and Ice rivers and up Boulder Creek. Fortunately for visitors today, his plan to extract sodalite from the bed of the Ice River proved too expensive to be practical.

The first ambitious mining project in Yoho was started by the Pioneering Mining Company in the Ottertail River in 1885. The galena mine showed promise, but the valley was apparently not yet up to this kind of resource extraction. In 1887 a fire destroyed the stamp mill, sawmill, and store, along with the homes of the miners. The mine never reopened. The Monarch Mine, however, was a different story.

British Columbia Smelting Company Limited was incorporated in London, England, May 8, 1888. At the end of that year, the company had already built a

The Monarch Mine. (Photograph courtesy Canadian Parks Service.)

133

smelter in Vancouver and was ready to take advantage of the newly opened railway to bring the lead and silver it took out of Mt. Stephen to the minerals market. Overestimating the production of the mine, the company was in financial trouble by 1889 and had to sell its Vancouver smelter. The mine in Field closed down. Later in 1889, the Galena Mining and Smelting Company in Calgary debated about putting a smelter in Field but decided instead to build it in Golden. Because of the unreliability of the mine, it, too, proved disastrous and the company soon failed. Little happened at the Monarch Mine for the next 16 years. In the meantime, mining operations were largely concentrated in the Ice River area, where iron, zinc, and galena were extracted briefly from the Shining Beauty Mine.

In the summer of 1906, the Monarch Mine got a new lease on life when the Canadian Concentrating and Smelting Company built new accommodations for miners below Mt. Stephen and installed a wire tramway up the mountain. Since the first ore extracted showed promise, a gravity tramway was constructed from the CPR tracks to a new tunnel portal, which it was hoped, would lead to the richest veins of ore. This tramway, which climbed up the steep cliffs of the lower shoulders of Mt. Stephen, offered precarious views of the abyss below. Early mining reports do not begin to tell how dangerous this place was. This report on the site was prepared by F. H. Bacon, Acting Gold Commissioner for the Province of British Columbia in 1910:

> At this point the railway curves around the shoulder of a precipitous bluff, and the outcrop of ore on which the mine was located was discovered …on the face of the bluff, 700 feet vertically above tunnel No. 134, on the Canadian Pacific Railway. The outcrop seems almost inaccessible, but was reached from a slide to the eastward by building, along the face of the cliff, a gallery, supported on brackets bolted on to the rocks, to the outcrop of ore on the face of the cliff. From the outcrop a tunnel was driven in on a vein for some distance, and, according to report, a well-defined vein was followed and a considerable body of ore found.

In 1910 the mine shipped 48 tonnes of ore to the refinery it reopened in Golden. In 1916, the Monarch Mine was sold to Great West Mines Company of Vancouver, which took advantage of increased wartime demand for lead and zinc to accelerate production. This activity, however, was brief. By 1918, the mine was once again closed. In 1924, the mine was again opened by a new mining consortium called the Pacific Mining Development and Petroleum Company. The company invested a great deal of money into state-of-the-industry extraction technology and new smelting processes. Production increased significantly. In 1929, the Monarch Mine was sold for the last time to Base Metals Mining Corporation, which took over both the Monarch and its sister across the valley, the Kicking Horse Mine on the lower shoulders of Mt. Field. From 1929 to 1935, Base Metals Mining doubled the size of the mine and extracted 232 192 tonnes of ore for smelting. Before it closed in 1952, it employed over 200 people who lived in a small community at the foot of Mt. Stephen not far from where the Cathedral Mountain chalets are found today. It was not until May 1968 that title to the mine property finally reverted to the national park and the mining era officially came to an end in Yoho.

Logging

Hector's earliest descriptions of the Kicking Horse Valley give ample indication of just how thick the forests on the west side of the Great Divide were in the mid-19th century. That same dense vegetation, however, proved enormously valuable to a railroad in need of timber for ties, bridges, and buildings. The first timber berths permitted in what is now Yoho National Park were granted in the years 1884, 1886, and 1887 to help the railway complete its main line through Kicking Horse Pass. Later, trees were also cut to build section stations, telegraph lines, bunk houses, hotels, townsites, and attendant roads and bridges.

The federal government was forced to issue timber rights all over the park. Although these leases, or "lesses," were granted for only one year, they were almost automatically renewable as long as merchantable forest still existed on the land and the land was not required for settlement. A timber berth could be of any shape and size and could be up to 65 square kilometres (25 square miles) in area. By the 1890s, 117 timber berths were licensed in the railway belt and dozens more were scattered along the perimeter. It was not until 1906 that forests were protected in any effective way in British Columbia.

A later reduction in the area of Yoho National Park and the adoption of the National Parks Act in 1930 eliminated all the major timber berths from the park except those in the Amiskwi Valley. In 1948, owners of logging licences were faced with either operating these berths or permanently relinquishing logging rights in the park. G. Elliott, holder of the remaining major timber leases, opted to cut the merchantable timber in the Amiskwi Valley and contracted with National Forests Products to do the work. The camp for the mill on Harrison Creek grew quickly into a small village with a population of nearly 300 people. At peak times the logging company employed 130. Before it burned down in 1953 and the children were bussed into Field, the Amiskwi school had as many as 32 students in attendance. By the time the timber berth was exhausted in 1969, it is calculated that more than 80 million board feet of lumber had been hauled out of the Amiskwi Valley.

Meanwhile, the park was trying valiantly not to lose more forests to fire. By 1940, Yoho National Park had been divided into four districts, with Warden

Service headquarters in each. District wardens were stationed in the centre of these districts, at Hector (near Wapta Lake), in Field, at Ottertail, and at Leanchoil. Assistant wardens were hired for the summer at Takakkaw Falls and at Lake O'Hara. Three fire lookouts — on Mt. Hunter, Mt. King, and Mt. Paget — were staffed each summer.

"Two Gun" Joe Burkitt

Early park wardens were often real characters. Joe Burkitt was such a character. After meeting his wife, Mamie, in England during World War I, he returning to Canada with his young bride and settled in Kaslo, British Columbia. In 1923, Burkitt took a job with the parks service in Yoho. Since accommodation was hard to find in Field, the Burkitts resided for a time in the Railway Y before moving into a tent adjacent to the blacksmith's house across the river. In 1929, Burkitt became a park warden in Yoho under the direction of Dick Langford.

"Two Gun" Joe Burkitt established a reputation for himself by wearing matching pistols as part of his park warden uniform. Here Joe is saying goodbye to his son Doug who is about to go off to fight in the Second World War. (Photograph courtesy of the Burkitt family.)

He was ultimately responsible for the Wapta and Ottertail districts of the park. The work of the park warden was as varied then as it is now. Burkitt was responsible for fire protection, policing of poachers, maintaining telephone lines, trail maintenance, mountain rescue, and bear control. It was in this latter capacity that Joe Burkitt earned his nickname.

After some years in the service of National Parks, Burkitt began carrying two revolvers in a holster around his waist, gunfighter style. One day, it is reported, Burkitt walked out of the park office in Field only to confront a black bear wandering around in front of the Monarch Hotel. Burkitt calmly pulled both pistols from their holsters and shot a number of rounds over the head of the bear to scare it out of town. Blowing the smoke out of the hot barrels, he just as calmly replaced them in their holsters and continued on his way. In 1950, Burkitt moved his family to Revelstoke where he continued to work as a park warden in Mt. Revelstoke, and Glacier national parks until he retired in 1959.

Fourteen years after my nephew married a sprightly Revelstoke girl, I discovered she was the grand-daughter of "Two Gun" Joe Burkitt.

The Rutherfords

Since its inception, the National Parks has employed some very interesting and highly committed people in its service. Richard Langford, Jock Tocher, Jim Simes, Bill Hollingsworth, and Glen Brook were but a few who became legends during their service in Yoho National Park. A young man who grew up in the shadow of these legends was Gordon Rutherford. The youngest of a family of three children, Gordon was born in Salmon Arm, British Columbia, in December 1938. Gordon was only a small child when his father, Melbourne, brought his wife, Lillian, and the rest of his family to Field, where he worked as a machinist's helper on the stream trains. In July 1942, the family moved into the west apartment of the Strand Hotel. Smaller than Mt. Stephen House, small-

Bev and Gordon Rutherford.

er even than the Monarch Hotel across from the roundhouse, the Strand had only five apartment rooms, which were often let out to incoming railway workers until they could find a house in town. Gordon remembers that Field was a thriving community with a bake shop, butcher shop, two groceries, a hardware store, a post office, and six boarding houses. There was Legion Hall, a variety of service clubs, a teen town, and three churches. Although it was not as luxurious as the Banff Springs course, there was a golf course just west of town. When the elk were not on it, all eight or nine holes were available for play. There was even a ski area across from town, developed exclusively for locals. Although the highway had been completed through Yoho Park in the summer of 1927, there were still three passenger trains each way, running through Field. The Kicking Horse and Monarch mines were operating under the name of Base Metal Mines, and logging was still being done in the park.

Since Mel Rutherford knew everyone who worked with the railway in Field, young Gordon was on familiar terms with even the most famous railroaders. Gordon's great-uncle Wally, who was an engineer on a pusher, was a close friend of Seth Partridge's. In 1922 Seth Partridge immortalized himself by heroically saving the lives of his fellow workers when a rock slide threatened the Mars section house below Cathedral Mountain. The railway renamed the section house after Partridge, and each day Partridge passed it as he herded a 5900 series locomotive up the Big Hill.

In the summer of 1955, at the age of 16, Rutherford got a summer trail crew job with Yoho National Park. That summer Gordon received a thorough introduction to the backcountry of the Hector District, which included Yoho Valley, the Little Yoho Valley, and the Lake O'Hara area. One day Gordon found himself in the upper reaches of the Yoho Valley with a senior warden named Glen Brook. Brook had begun his career with the National Parks Warden Service at Marble Canyon in Kootenay in 1946. In 1955 Brook had brought his wife, Irene, to Yoho, where he was soon to become the park's chief warden. At Twin Falls, Brook had discovered that debris had fallen from a scree slope above Twin Falls Creek and blocked one side of the falls. To Glen Brook's knowledge, this had not happened since the summer of 1910, when Swiss guides had cleared out a similar rock and gravel jam that changed the course of the stream. To prevent the famous falls from being changed, Brook instructed Rutherford to help clear the blocked channel. Rutherford and his companions on the trail crew scooped out the gravel obstructing the course of the creek with their hands.

Rutherford met another Yoho legend that summer in Slim Haugen, the park's horse packer, ferrier, blacksmith, and sometimes-warden who lived at the Yoho Ranch just west of Field. Haugen had come to Field in the summer of 1949 and for many years was considered one the national park system's most competent horse trainers. Slim's last posting before he retired from his long career with the parks service was at the Ya-HaTinda Ranch, where he raised horses for use in all the mountain national parks.

In the summer of 1955, Twin Falls creek was partially blocked by a scree slide off the slope above the Whaleback Trail. The trail crew was instructed to remove the debris from the creek to allow the famous falls to continue its course. The work was done by hand as it was when the falls stopped once before in 1910. (Photographs courtesy of Glen Brook.)

In the summer of 1956, Rutherford returned to his trail crew job in the Hector District. One of his duties that summer was to help the Hector District park warden Noel Gardiner fill the cistern at Paget Lookout with snow so that the fire spotter who worked there for the summer had a reliable source of water. Later that summer, Rutherford witnessed firsthand how long exposure to the solitude of the park could affect one's creativity. To prevent boredom, Glen Brook had instructed the Paget fire lookout, Steve Hornyk, to paint the lookout house and its outbuilding. When Rutherford arrived one day to deliver supplies to Hornyk, he discovered that Hornyk had painted both the outside and the inside of the lookout green. Hornyk had also painted colourful flowers on the chimney, the stovepipe, the kettle, and the teapot. Outside he had painted little green trees on the flagstones leading to the outhouse and on the rock faces on the short cliffs that rose above the lookout.

Gordon Rutherford decided to stay on. He became a permanent warden in June 1961 and worked that summer at Leanchoil under well-respected district warden Fred Dixon. With a promising career in the offing, Gordon married Beverly Staples on July 1 of that same year. By the time I met him in the summer of 1978, Gordon and Bev had lived and worked in three of the park's four districts before the district system was changed and warden operations were centred in Field. Rutherford would introduce me to Glen Brook, who had since retired from the Warden Service, and between them and another Yoho warden named Dale Portman, I would be formally introduced to the ways and the wonder of Yoho.

Field in Transition

When we arrived in Field, the life of the town was ebbing. The railway was moving more and more of its operations to Golden, and the future of the town was uncertain. The Canadian Parks Service was not sure whether it wanted a town like Field as a service centre, and the town's population was in decline. In 1979, the Monarch Hotel burned down, depriving the town of one of its last historical monuments and its only remaining watering hole. Later the aging curling rink burned down, too.

A decade later, the town's future looked much brighter. Although few railway workers remained in town, the parks service had granted permission for people who worked in Lake Louise to own homes in Field. New houses slowly began to replace the tinysalt boxes that had been constructed out of scrapped railway cars at the turn of the 20th century. A new visitor centre brought people off the highway.and the fossil beds above and adjacent to the town were bringing international attention to Field.

The town and the park remind us of how quickly our world can change. When Mt. Stephen Park was set aside in the Kicking Horse Valley more than a century ago, the West was almost wilderness. Now the national parks along the railway belt in British Columbia are just tiny islands surrounded by industry, development, and private land. The 8-car passenger trains have been replaced by grain trains almost 2 kilometers long. Millions of people now drive through Yoho every year on the Trans-Canada Highway, many of them barely noticing the national park around them. And yet the wonder of Yoho precariously survives. The rock walls and the waterfalls come to life with each passing spring. The forests creak and mumble in the wind. Wildflowers blossom in the high meadows, through which the last of the great bears wander in search of food and mates. Sun-exposed rock shatters. The mountains are crumbling. Beneath the bruised blue shoulders of Mt. Stephen, Field shimmers in the brief, fierce heat of summer. In the silence between each passing train, in the stillness between each breeze, the past speaks. It tells us that we are what we remember. Our lives are shaped and given value by how well we understand our pasts. In this national park our history is still all there for us to see.

"It is wonderful," the Native people said. Yoho, the name for wonder.

A low point in the life of the town of Field happened when the Monarch Hotel burned down in 1979. The town, however, rebounded and even became prosperous again.

The Burgess Shales are located high above the Wapta Traverse, a trail extending below Mt. Wapta all the way to Burgess Pass. It is high, steep and exposed country.

Dr. Desmond Collins is one of the world's experts on the life of the Cambrian seas. He works with the Royal Ontario Museum and has been studying the Burgess Shales for more than a decade.

Though trilobites like this one are the best known of the Cambrian fossils, other fossils forms are beginning to tell us more about the significance of the Burgess shales to our understanding of the history of life on Earth.

Epilogue

The Most Famous Fossils in the World

Campbell's Ordinary Soup Does Make Peter Pale. I am sitting in the Siding General Store in Field trying to use Stephen Jay Gould's mnemonic device for remembering the geological periods of the Paleozoic Epoch of the earth's history. I have returned to Field to take a course sponsored by the Friends of Yoho National Park Society on the natural history of the park's world-famous fossils. The course is being offered by Desmond Collins, a prominent paleontologist from the Royal Ontario Museum. I am gradually making sense out of the soup. Cambrian. Ordovician. Silurian. Devonian. Mississippian. Pennsylvanian. Permian. In contrast to the city, you can sit at the table in this general store and not be bothered, not even by the staff. There is no urban-style customer service focus. The cook only comes to the counter to serve customers when it is convenient to interrupt the making of chocolate chip cookies. A woman enters wearing a print dress, grey wool work socks with a red line around the toes, and Birkenstock sandals on her feet. Although a couple of customers are waiting at the counter, she bypasses them to talk to the cook, who is now slicing tomatoes for sandwiches. Although I have not lived in Field for more than 10 years, I gratefully realize that the pace of the town has not changed.

The Burgess Shales course, offered by the Friends of Yoho Society, is held in the auditorium of the recently condemned school. It is no matter, however. A number of national institutions have been vying to help the town build an educational centre around the United Nations World Heritage Site on the slopes between Mt. Wapta and Mt. Field, where the most complete Cambrian fossils known in the world were discovered by Charles Doolittle Walcott at roughly the same time as the Spiral Tunnels were completed on the Big Hill.

Although it is a fiercely bright summer day, all the doors are closed so that Dr. Collins can show his slides. Between 1972 and 1992, Collins has spent 10 field seasons in the Burgess Shales. He is considered one of the world experts on these fossils and on the life of the Cambrian seas. People from all over western Canada have come to Field to hear him speak and to join this field trip to excavations he and his party were currently making in the Burgess Shales. One couple has also come from the United States to hear Collins speak. The course begins casually with lots of coffee and an introduction to a variety of fossil discoveries made in the park since the beds were discovered.

Collins easily recounts that during the construction of Mt. Stephen House, one of the carpenters working on the building went prospecting on Mt. Stephen and discovered "stone bugs." He showed them to surveyor Otto Klotz, who later showed them to geologist R. G. McConnell of the Geological Survey of Canada and to State of Michigan geologist Karl Rominger, who published descriptions of the ancient life forms in a technical journal in 1887. Charles Walcott, who was an avid collector of fossils,though he had no formal training in geology, read Rominger's article. When the great mountaineer Edward Whymper came to the Rockies in the summer of 1901, he too visited the famous Mt. Stephen fossils beds to look at what were increasingly seen as the oldest fossils in the world. That same summer, Whymper arranged the construction of a trail from Emerald Lake to the summit of Yoho Pass and along the Wapta Traverse to Burgess Pass. In 1907, Charles Walcott, who had advanced to the prestigious position of Secretary of the Smithsonian in Washington, D.C., came to Mt. Stephen to collect some of the stone-frozen Cambrian critters. While he was in Field, Arthur Wheeler, the president of the Alpine Club of Canada, invited him to write an article on his finds. In 1909, Walcott and his second wife, Helen, came to the Rockies for a working holiday. While traversing Whymper's trail across the middle slopes of Mt. Wapta, they discovered a second great fossil bed now known as the Burgess Shales.

A half hour into the introduction, many in the audience were suddenly struck by the realization that this course was going to offer far more than they ever could have expected. Beyond Dr. Collins's elegant lecturing style resided a profound love of human history that was equalled only by his encyclopedic understanding of time frozen into stone in the Burgess Shales. His presentation embraced a thorough and insightful biography of Charles Walcott and an assessment of his contribution to the science of his time. The program then went on to identify Walcott's major fossil discoveries and to trace the interpretation of these discoveries, through much upheaval in thought, to the present. Collins then subtly placed before his audience a professional point of view about the significance of the Burgess fossils based on his own highly respected work. It became clear that Dr. Collins's highly considered analysis of the Yoho's Cambrian fossils is at slight variance with the interpretations of Stephen Jay Gould offered in the popular book on the shales entitled Wonderful Life. This added a further dimension to the lively debate on the subject. Nonetheless, Collins concluded his lecture magnificently with a stunning summation of Gould's major point about the Burgess fossils and the evolution of life on earth. "Gould is right," Dr. Collins explained. "Contingency is a powerful evolutionary force. Natural calamities may well be powerful agents in the wholesale elimination of life forms. Extinction of even the most evolved life forms is possible. If it happened in the past — next time it could be our turn." With this remark, the room was stilled by a silence that seemed to last for ages.